Miniature Needlepoint and Sewing Projects for Dollhouses

Miniature rooms at Mini Mundus shop. Photograph by Jay Goode. Courtesy of *New York Magazine*.

Miniature Needlepoint and Sewing Projects for Dollhouses

by KATHRYN FALK
and the Staff of Mini Mundus

Photographs by Sydnie Michel

Hawthorn Books, Inc.
Publishers/New York
A Howard & Wyndham Company

To my father, Bernie V. Falk,
who always gave me love and encouragement

MINIATURE NEEDLEPOINT AND SEWING PROJECTS FOR DOLLHOUSES

Library of Congress Catalog Card Number: 76–53393
ISBN: 0–8015–5073–4
1 2 3 4 5 6 7 8 9 10

Contents

4 Kay Sobers's Needlepoint Specialities

5 Window Treatments

6 Inhabitants of Dollhouses

7 Accessories

Acknowledgments

To the staff of Mini Mundus: Kit Cox, Nan Fishman, Lois Powers, Jewel Richards, Terry Rogal, and Neil Rosenburg. Everlasting gratitude for managing to keep the Mini Mundus school, shop, and lumberyard from falling apart one inch by one foot!

To my psychiatrists, who kept my ego from being reduced to the size of my miniature furniture, thank you forever.

To Mickey Benamy, Barbara Hackney, Bonnie McLean, Robert Milne, Norm Nelson, and Dorothy Wade: my deepest appreciation for your cooperation over the past year.

To Len Mizerek and Haydee Verdia for their wonderful drawings.

A very special thanks to Frederick Decker for support and cooperation.

Miniature Needlepoint and Sewing Projects for Dollhouses

1
Introduction to Miniature Settings

An exquisite miniature setting depends on its accessories. A room usually needs a rug or a sofa, draperies or curtains, not to mention countless other furnishings. Expressing your own tastes makes decorating a dollhouse or miniature room a fascinating hobby.

At Mini Mundus we have a corps of sewing and needlepoint experts who create fine, perfectly detailed handiwork. Now that miniatures have become the third biggest hobby in America, they are busier than ever. This book was compiled in order to let you in on many of their secrets, and to present projects that will help you to provide the perfect finishing touches to your miniature rooms.

It is really very easy to decorate a dollhouse. Start by looking around your own house. The one you live in.

There's probably clothing hanging in the closet, slippers under the bed, a nightgown in the dresser drawer, towels in the bathroom, a potholder in the kitchen, and place mats on the dining room table. If you don't have curtains on the windows, then you probably have shades or blinds. Is there a mat on the bathroom floor? Throw pillows on your upholstered sofa? Or do you ever dream of furnishings, such as a canopy bed or an oriental carpet?

Begin your planning by studying your favorite rooms; consult magazines, such as *House and Garden Decorating Guide* or *Antique*, to discover what your favorite setting would include.

Miniature room setting (interior by Terry Rogal). Clothespin dolls from the
collection of Jane Howarth.

Then miniaturize your favorite pieces to a scale of 1″ to 1′
(more about that later).

The result, when it is all complete, providing you have
patience, will be a near-perfect setting.

As a consolation for your patience, the room will always
remain just as you want it to be. Your tiny things will hardly
ever gather dust (when you find out what to do!). More impor-
tantly, no one will cause a cigarette burn, spill wine, tear the
upholstery, or walk on the rug with muddy shoes!

There are some basic rules of thumb that will help smooth
your way. Most miniature pieces are scaled 1″ to 1′. This means
that if a man is six feet tall, the male doll should be approximately
six inches tall. If a sofa is five feet wide, it will be five inches wide
in the dollhouse. There are other scales, ¾″ to 1′, ½″ to 1′, etc.,
but since 90 percent of the dollhouses and pieces of furniture and
accessories are scaled 1″ to 1′, you will have difficulty finding
furnishings in any other scale.

A good way to protect your miniatures is to have a façade or
panel doors hinged to the front of your house, or to fit a sliding
glass panel over the opening.

One fastidious miniature collector and dollhouse builder, Margaret Styne, has an acute aversion to dust collecting in her dollhouses. She makes certain that the windows are tightly sealed and has designed special Plexiglas fronts on her houses that fit tight as a drum and are easy to remove. As she says, "Who wants to wield a paintbrush every week in order to keep rooms dusted!" (If your collection does collect dust—remember that a tiny paintbrush is the cleaning tool!) Margaret's husband, Jule Styne, wrote the miniature collector's theme song, "Small World, Isn't It?"

Aside from dust, I caution you against cats, visiting children, overly curious adults, and particularly, the suction from a vacuum cleaner. Many a treasure has been dropped or has completely disappeared.

Another product that you won't be able to exist without is Mini Hold. It costs $2 and is a little can of wax that acts as a temporary adhesive. Without Mini Hold, you are constantly knocking over pieces—and losing them—especially when there are lids on cookie jars and teapots. It also holds up pictures, holds

Kathryn Falk at Mini Mundus lumberyard.

down place mats and napkins, keeps everything in order, and even helps in draping curtains. The best part is that if you are careful you can remove the residue of wax from wallpapers and tabletops when you decide to redecorate and rearrange your things.

PREPARATION

Once you have decided on the style of a room, be it a romantic French pink-and-white bedroom, eighteenth-century living room, or country kitchen with brass pots and pans, don't settle for less than exactly what you want. Let your miniature setting be a total reflection of your tastes.

Design interpretation is an important element. Before deciding upon what kind of needlework accessories you want for a room, be it a petit point rug or a crocheted afghan, make certain that it fits in with the rest of your decor and color scheme.

Gather some photos of favorite examples. Place the photos across the room from where you are sitting. Look for the strongest elements in the design—the *ones that repeat* and the *strongest colors* in the pattern.

A simple pattern of geometric shapes that repeats and inter-repeats will give a much better miniature effect than an elaborately involved design. Dark colors give depth, and when used strategically against medium and pale tones, they can take the place of several shades.

When purchasing threads for a sewing project, choose a full selection of colors and shades that match your decor. Bring them home and experiment with color samples. Work a small sample and place them in the miniature room to see how it harmonizes. Working samples will ensure fewer mistakes in the final product. It is time and energy well spent.

A good, relaxed working situation is important. You need excellent light, either natural light or a 100-watt soft white bulb directed at the work in the hands. Don't use a table light! A flexible arm lamp is recommended. Pose it above your head, not in your eyes.

Bonnie McLean, the Mini Mundus needlepoint expert, makes the following recommendations: Keep your hands very clean and dry. The slightest moisture and perspiration makes the needle grab and slows down your work. Moisture in your hand also softens the canvas, which can cause distortion.

When you do canvas work, place a dark cloth across your lap so you can see the holes in the canvas better.

Sit in a comfortable straight-back chair that makes you sit with good posture. Work with your elbows close to your sides.

A magnifying mirror can be helpful. There are several good models available at needlework and art supply shops. The Bausch and Lomb magnifiers from Charrette, in New York City, are reasonably priced for approximately $20 and up.

When starting a miniature needlework project, work one-half hour at a time and then go back to regular activities. This gives your eye muscles a chance to adjust to this new type of exercise. Work up gradually to longer periods of work. When your eyes feel tired, you should stop for a while or you will find your patience and interest easily drained, not to mention the fading of your eyesight if overstrained.

When threading a needle, if the thread seems to spread apart at the end when fitting it through the eye, try the other end of the thread. One end is always easier to thread than the other. If that doesn't work, clip the end off and try again. Make sure the needle is the proper size.

As you are working, your thread will start to curl up. When it does this, hold the needlework up and let the thread dangle. It will uncurl itself. For neat work and rhythmic stitching, this is essential.

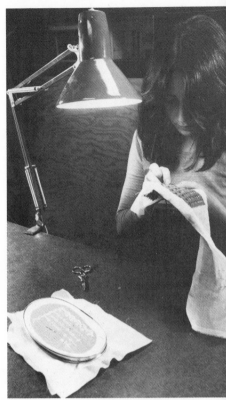

Bonnie McLean using a flexible arm lamp.

Left: Dottie Gulker using goose-necked magnifying glass while crocheting.

Dorothy Wade using Luxo illuminated magnifying glass to create miniature furniture.

MATERIALS

Here is a list of basic tools. Specific tools will be included in individual instructions.

Scissors

Use small, sharp, finely pointed scissors (see photo page 120). Cut every thread. Never break threads. Threads cut with dull scissors are too hard to thread through tiny needles.

Needles

Different needles are used for different types of work. Small crewel needles are best for petit point and bargello; sharps are necessary for sewing such as appliqué. It is most important to use the proper size needle for your thread and material. When threaded, the right size needle will slide back and forth on the thread without catching but will not fall from the thread by itself. When the threaded needle is pulled through the fabric or canvas, it should not force the threads to spread apart as with a needle that is too large. If the needle goes through too easily but you feel it grab when it gets to the thread, the needle is too small.

Hoop

Use a small hoop, smaller in diameter than the size of your hand, to keep petit point canvas from distorting. Work with one hand underneath and one hand above, passing needle from one hand to the other.

Threads

Use the best quality threads. Low-quality threads are no end of trouble. They kink and snarl and shred. This produces a low-quality, uneven product and means hours spent in useless aggravation. Keep your threads short. Never cut a thread more than twelve or fifteen inches long. Never double over threads. Never use knots at the ends of threads. Either weave the thread into the back of the fabric (four or five running stitches) or take one or two short backstitches putting the needle through the previous backstitch. Once they are secure, cut threads close. End the same way. All threads must be colorfast. Make certain that whatever ply you use covers the canvas completely and passes through the holes with ease. If you don't live near a needlework shop, in order to get an estimate of the amount of thread you need for a project,

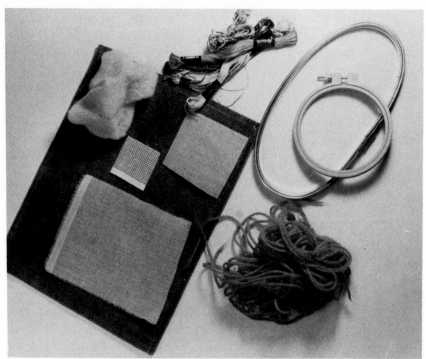
Sewing and needlepoint materials.

work a square inch in the type of stitch and with the materials you plan to use. Then you can estimate the amount of thread needed by multiplying the amount used in the sample by the number of square inches in that particular color. Make certain that you have enough thread because dye lots change and it is hard to match colors at a later date.

A knowledge of the most popular needlework materials will help when you order by mail or buy in a needlework shop.

The D.M.C. crochet and embroidery threads have an excellent finish that allows you to pull the stitches tighter, a necessity in miniature needlepoint projects. They are also perfect for sewing stitches on miniature lace and appliquéing. These imported threads have more mellow colors and there are approximately 200 shades of them.

THREE-STRAND PERSIAN WOOL. Sometimes sold by the skein and sometimes by the length, it is a good source for needlepoint rugs. It is easy to use one or more strands at once, depending on the size of your canvas. If you don't want to work with wool, try *silk or cotton thread* for your miniature rugs.

APPLETON AND MEDICI PETIT POINT WOOL. These brands are not as available as the Persian wool but they have a high quality and more consistency.

Canvases

MONO CANVAS OR REGULAR COTTON NEEDLEPOINT CANVAS. This canvas comes in sizes 5 mesh to 24. We don't recommend less than 18 mesh canvas for rugs, otherwise the finished product is very bulky and thick.

PENELOPE CANVAS. This is the most popular canvas for petit point. It is stiff, with the thread woven in pairs. On a 10 mesh Penelope canvas, if you make the stitch over the pair of woven canvas stitches, you have a 10-stitch Penelope. If you go over each stitch, you have a 20-stitch Penelope.

SILK CANVAS. This is best for upholstering your needlework. It is very expensive but fine quality, and comes in 36 to 56 mesh. The higher the number, the more difficult it is to work. An alternative, in miniature upholstering, is the Penelope canvas.

TECHNIQUES

Upholstery

When you furnish a miniature setting, you will find that there is a scarcity of fine upholstered pieces available. If you are going to create an exquisite setting, which is what most of us aspire to, you will either have to commission one of the handful of miniature upholstery specialists (listed under "Custom Work" in the Appendix), wait perhaps a year or two because they are usually back-ordered, and pay a goodly sum, or you can learn to create upholstered furniture on your own.

If you don't care to work from scratch, and you have no intentions of using a saw, there are a variety of kits for you that need only to be assembled. They are described at the end of each chapter.

If it is your confidence that needs bolstering in order to do upholstering, practice learning the rudimentary techniques on one of the kits. Then move ahead, utilizing that 1790 fabric that a friend at the museum was able to obtain for you, or any antique or new fabric as long as it is *lightweight* and the *pattern is small*. They make the best upholstery materials.

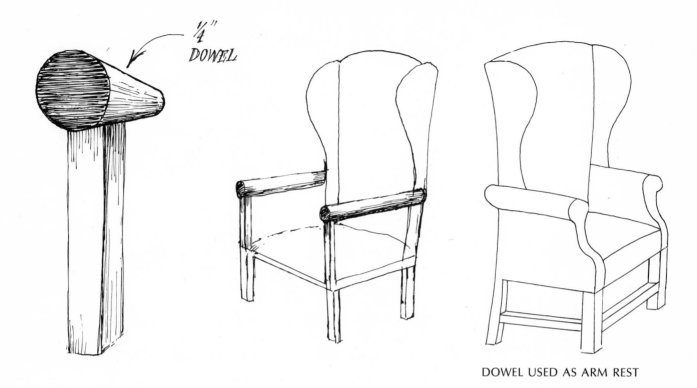

¼" DOWEL

DOWEL USED AS ARM REST

Basically, the format is very simple. You just need to choose the right materials and have a dose of patience.

You select a pattern. Cut out the back, the seat, and the sides, using ³⁄₃₂" or ⅛" basswood. (Some people prefer cardboard for the back and sides.)

If you wish, add a ¼" dowel to the top of the side pieces to create the arm rests. Glue on enough padding to achieve the desired shape and then upholster.

If the front of the seat is to be curved, glue a shaped piece of wood to the front edge. Cover the seat unit with upholstery fabric, pulling it tautly over the front and gluing it to the underside of the base. You may or may not add a seat cushion.

Upholstering a piece of furniture is not performed as in actual life. Corners generally need to be mitered to avoid lumps. The least overlapping—even if it means snipping away excess fabric—gives the best results.

There is no sewing. Fabric coverings are glued on. To hide seams, glue on decorative welting of tiny cords, or braided flosses and threads. Avoid patterns that are large; they must look in proper scale! Thick and bulky fabrics are hopeless. Be extra careful using velvet—a glue spot, either from your fingers or an excess dab on a seam spilling over—will leave a stain.

If you don't want to attempt carving cabriole legs, they are now available ready-made from X-acto.

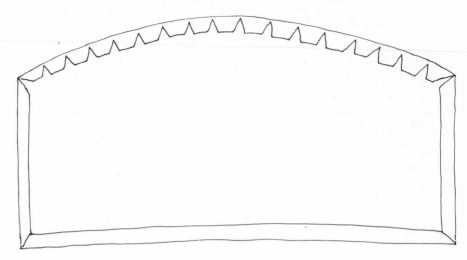

MITERING A CURVED AREA

READY-MADE CABRIOLE
LEG FROM X-ACTO

General Directions for Working with Wood

If you have chosen to use the 1″-to-1′ scale, follow the patterns as given, unless indicated otherwise. An architect's ruler or the 1″-to-1′ ruler is a must.

SELECT THE WOOD. Start with soft basswood, then progress to mahogany and hardwoods.

TRACE HALF THE PATTERN. Then fold the paper double, making very sure that the fold is square.

LAY OUT THE PATTERN ON THE WOOD. Draw on the wood with the grain, trace around your pattern for curved lines (always use metal ruler for straight lines).

TURNINGS. You don't have a lathe? Well, start filing round and round. It's slow.

HOLES FOR CHAIR LEGS. Drill them. Be wary of angles and don't drill through.

FINISHES. The stain must be used before you glue. Brush it on each piece, then wipe off and let dry. (MinWax brand stains are highly recommended.)

When the pieces are dry, carefully glue them together. (X-acto's tinted glue is wonderful.) Let the glue dry, then finish as you would for a natural finish.

NATURAL FINISH. Use shellac, cut 50 percent with denatured alcohol. Brush on, sand, and shellac again. Then rub down with very fine steel wool dipped in a little salad oil. Polish with a soft rag.

PAINT. Use model paint. If you spray paint, cut the side out of a carton and put the piece to be painted in it. This way you avoid a mess.

HELPFUL HINT. When cutting small or intricate pieces of wood, cut out an accurate paper pattern and glue it to the wood with rubber cement. Cut out the piece needed and then peel off the pattern and rub off any remaining cement.

Crocheting

If you have been hesitant about attempting miniature crocheted afghans, or attempting crocheting at all, there is an exciting new method for following instructions. It is called the Japanese symbol system for crocheting. The symbols are an abstraction of what the stitches look like, and they are much easier to follow than written instructions, which are often full of misprints.

The Mini Mundus crochet expert, Rebecca Mercer-White, discovered the system in San Francisco at Yo's Needlecraft. There you can find people of different nationalities, who speak a variety of languages, sitting around, following the symbol patterns, and turning out the same piece of work.

It is a good idea always to learn the technique in a large scale. Practice all the crochet stitches with big crochet hooks before attempting them in miniature. Find yourself a good yarn shop, one that will explain how to crochet, needlepoint, or whatever. All good shops have this service. Build up a good relationship. They will help you get started.

Rebecca makes the following suggestions: Aside from a yarn shop's supply, look for sewing thread. In most cases, sewing threads are more in scale. The smallest crochet yarn usually available is a smidgin too large but it gives a homespun effect. It is excellent for little curtains and bedspreads.

Make swatches of stitches before starting a project. Most people, after a few swatches, learn their gauge and then adopt it. Figure out how loose or tight you want it to be. Beginners have a tendency to pull the thread too tight.

Whenever possible, use good yarn. You can buy one skein and dye it different colors with Rit or vegetable dye.

You need a good hand to create tiny crocheted articles. Even

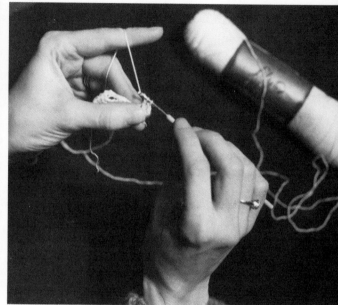
Close-up of crochet stitches.

Rebecca Mercer-White crocheting miniature curtains.

stitches and a relaxed hand are required. Try one square a day of the quilts, to promote consistency.

To create a lace effect, crochet loosely. Do not clip the ends of your piece too closely before stretching or they may pull out. Leave a lot of excess to weave in. When pulling a number of ends through, a needle or hook finer than the one used to crochet the piece will be much easier to insert in the stitches.

The joy of crocheting, in general, is that you are working with only one stitch at a time. You can change plans or correct mistakes as soon as you find them.

Don't forget the value of a *standing magnifying glass*, as described earlier in this chapter. For a small investment, you will find that crocheting in miniature is effortless.

Crochet Abbreviations

ch (chain)
sl st (slip stitch)
sc (single crochet)
hdc (half double crochet)
dc (double crochet)
trc (treble crochet)
st (stitch)
sp (space)

sk (skip)
beg (beginning)
rnd (round)
rep (repeat)
tog (together)
yo (h) (yarn over hook)
lp (loop)

It is possible for you to sketch and crochet patterns yourself, using the symbol method, and produce a drawing from the written instructions. You don't need a symbol, for instance, to skip 4 stitches. You see it pictorially.

Basic Stitches

Begin with *slipknot*.

CHAIN. Insert hook in loop, yarn over hook and pull through.

Slip knot

Japanese symbol

Chain stitch

SLIP STITCH. Insert hook in stitch, yarn over hook and pull through stitch and loop on hook at same time. This "slipping" is one way to leave a space, and also to finish off a piece.

Japanese symbol

Slip stitch

SINGLE CROCHET. Insert hook in stitch, yarn over hook and pull through stitch, yarn over hook and pull through both loops on hook.

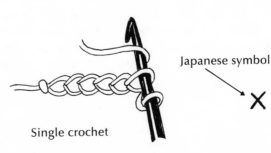

Japanese symbol

X

Single crochet

DOUBLE CROCHET. Yarn over hook, insert hook in stitch, pull through stitch (yarn over hook and pull through two loops) twice.

Double crochet

Japanese symbol

TREBLE CROCHET. Yarn over hook twice, insert hook in stitch, yarn over hook and pull through stitch (yarn over hook and pull through two loops) three times.

Treble crochet

Japanese symbol

HALF DOUBLE CROCHET. Yarn over hook, insert hook in stitch, yarn over hook, pull through stitch, yarn over hook and pull through all three loops on hook.

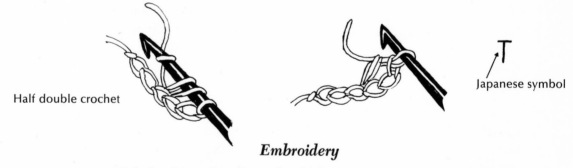

Half double crochet

Japanese symbol

Embroidery

Fabrics for embroidery should be of a linenlike weave. Allow a few inches extra all around size of finished embroidered piece as fabric has a tendency to ravel when being worked. Choose a needle that slips easily through the fabric.

Place fabric in hoop to keep fabric taut while working. Do not make knots to begin or end threads. To start a thread, leave an end on wrong side; later thread it into a needle and run it under a few stitches.

If it is necessary to press the embroidered piece, place it face down on a well-padded ironing board. Steam it with a steam iron, but do not let the weight of the iron flatten the embroidery. Allow it to dry completely before moving it.

Basic Stitches

BUTTONHOLE STITCH. The buttonhole stitch is the basis of all looped stitches. When used as an edging, it is called the blanket stitch.

Work from left to right, starting the stitch from the bottom to *A*. Hold the thread down with your thumb, and bring the needle and thread around to the right, inserting to *B*, and at a desired distance above *A*. Bring the point out over the loop very close to *A* for a closed buttonhole stitch, or farther away for the open buttonhole stitch. Try a long and short open buttonhole stitch. Turn the work on the side, varying the length and spacing of the stitches. Join the tops of every two stitches by putting the needle in at the same spot at *B*. Or slant one of a pair of stitches to the right at *B*, and cross the second stitch over the first by slanting it to the left.

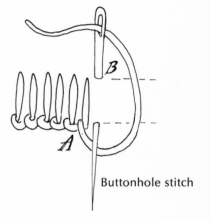

Buttonhole stitch

RUNNING STITCH. Work from right to left and make stitches even in size and spacing. Useful for outlining and as a foundation for composite stitches and for sewing tiny seams.

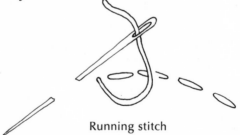

Running stitch

CHAIN STITCH. Working stitches from top down, bring needle to right side of fabric. Holding thread down with left thumb, insert needle back where thread emerged and bring out a short distance away; draw out needle over loop.

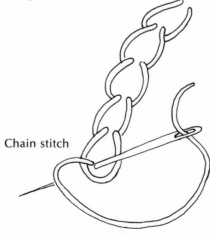

Chain stitch

Couching stitch

COUCHING STITCH. Lay the thread to be couched (sewn down by another thread) along the line of the design. With another thread, tie it down in even intervals with a small stitch into the fabric. You are actually appliquéing the thread. The couching thread can be of a contrasting color and thread type.

BLIND STITCH. This is used to join two fabrics together. Lay the top fabric with edge folded under on top of the other fabric. Stitch down with tiny stitches that go under the bottom fabric and come up just barely through the folded edge of the fabric being appliquéd.

Blind stitch

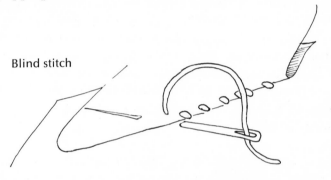

Satin stitch

SATIN STITCH. For filling where background fabric is to be covered completely. Bring needle up at one edge of area to be covered, insert needle at opposite edge, and return to starting line by carrying it underneath fabric. Make stitches close enough together to cover background fabric completely. Satin stitches should not be so long that they look loose and untidy.

HERRINGBONE (or Double Back) STITCH. Work from left to right. Bring needle up at *A*, insert at *B*, bring needle out at *C*; then insert at *D*, bring out at *E*.

Run stitches along parallel guidelines, either imaginary or drawn with a pencil, picking up a small amount of the fabric. Start from the left, working from left to right. The underside of the work shows little thread, so it is especially adaptable to transparent fabric. When closely worked within spaces between stitches, the Herringbone stitch looks like a variation of the Satin stitch.

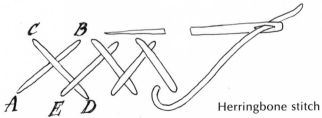

Herringbone stitch

LAZY DAISY STITCH. Bring thread up in center of "flower." Hold thread down with thumb; insert needle close to or in exact spot where thread emerged and bring out desired distance below; draw through over working thread. Then tie down with a tiny stitch made over loop as shown. Make similar stitches to form a circle around same center point.

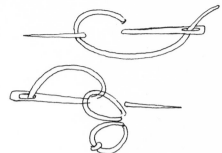

Lazy daisy stitch

OUTLINE STITCH. Also called stem or crewel stitch. For outlines, stems, and any fine line. Work from left to right. Bring needle up at end of line to be covered. Insert needle a short distance to the right and bring out a little way to the left at a slight angle. Keep thread above needle.

Outline stitch

Needlepoint Basic Stitches

CONTINENTAL STITCH. The continental stitch fully covers the back of the work. Work rows from right to left. Bring the needle up at 1; crossing the intersection diagonally, insert the needle at 2. Bring the needle up at 3, to the left of 1. Work in horizontal rows, turning the canvas upside down for each new row.

This stitch gives the nicest stitch for petit point and needlepoint, but distorts the canvas. So use this stitch only where you have a straight single row or an outline to follow.

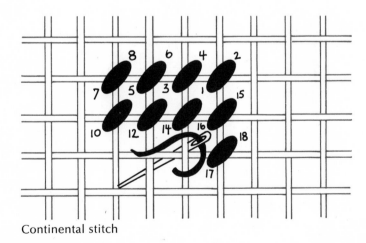

Continental stitch

BASKET-WEAVE STITCH. In appearance, the basket-weave stitch is the same as the continental. However, it is worked in diagonal rows rather than horizontally or vertically, resulting in a firm construction and an even regularity. This stronger construction lessens the tendency of the canvas to stretch out of shape. The work does not have to be turned upside down for each row.

Begin the first row at the lower right-hand corner of the canvas and proceed diagonally upward, bringing the needle in and out horizontally for each new stitch on the way upward, and in and out vertically on the following row as it proceeds downward.

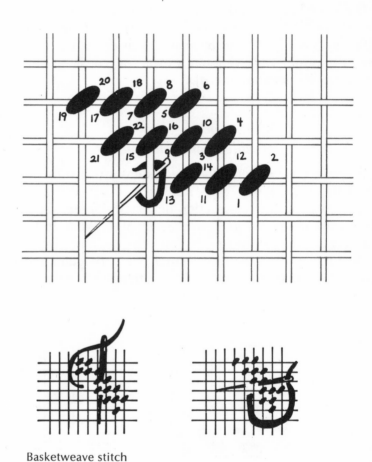

Basketweave stitch

HUNGARIAN POINT. This is a very simple bargello stitch. All the stitches are the same size and run vertically on the canvas. The stitches are worked over an even number of cross threads on the canvas. Rows of stitches run in zigzags, creating a vertical brick effect. Each new stitch starts halfway up the last.

When working stitches, hold canvas upright when you work up to the peak, and turn it around when you work down from the peak. This way you are always working the needle in the same direction.

Hungarian point has a much flatter effect than petit point because the rows are staggered. It is easier to visualize and it is quicker and easier to count. It is particularly suited to geometric designs. When worked in cotton or rayon floss there is virtually

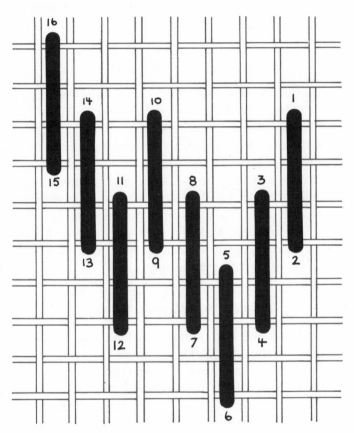

Hungarian point stitch

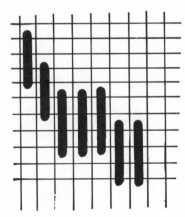

Flame stitch

no distortion. It can be worked without a hoop if stitches are pulled evenly and embroidery threads, running across the back of the canvas, are not picked up with new stitches. Because most of the stitch is on the face of the canvas, Hungarian point rugs are not so thick and lie closer to the floor. It also requires less yarn.

When working with stranded floss on canvas, weave ends into the back of completed areas and clip close when starting and finishing a thread. Loose ends of floss find their way to the face of the canvas when you work adjoining areas.

Blocking Needlepoint

After you have finished stitching your miniature piece it must be cleaned and blocked. Soak it in cold water and Woolite. Next, turn it upside down on a blocking surface tacked with brown paper. Mark the outline of the size you want the rug to be. Making sure the corners are straight and true, thumbtack the canvas, right side down, to the blocking board, through the unworked part of the canvas. When it is completely dry (after forty-eight hours), remove it from the board. It should remain rectangular; if not, repeat the blocking process. Make fringes: They can be hooked onto the last row of canvas with a crochet hook, making single loops. Then cut with scissors and trim evenly.

Binding Needlepoint Rugs

Rugs can be bound with single-fold bias tape the same color as the stitching on the edge. Take the piece of bias tape, open one fold, and stitch along the crease to the edge of the needlepoint. Trim the canvas about ⅜". Turn the bias tape down and topstitch over the bias tape seam. Turn in on the edge of the embroidery and steam press. Blindstitch to the canvas, making sure that the stitches don't go through the top of the embroidery. An alternative is that the rug can be lined and fringed like the oriental carpet in the "Needlepoint" chapter.

2

Living Room Treatments

HALL SETTEE

Materials

Padding (either foam rubber or polyester fiber)
Sobo glue
X-acto knife, miter box, and razor saw
Power scroll saw or jeweler's saw
Fabric (satin or brocade)
MinWax stain
1 sheet basswood, $\frac{1}{8}'' \times 4''$
1 sheet basswood, $\frac{1}{16}'' \times 4''$
1 strip basswood, $\frac{1}{8}'' \times \frac{3}{16}''$

1. Cut out the pieces of strip wood for the legs to the dimensions shown in the plans and assemble them.
2. Stain with MinWax and set aside to dry.
3. Cut out back and bottom from the $\frac{1}{8}'' \times 4''$ stock.
4. Cut out the back cushion and bottom cushion from the $\frac{1}{16}'' \times 4''$ stock.
5. With Sobo glue the padding material to the back and bottom cushions and set aside to dry.
6. Upholster the back and bottom, taking care to miter the corners and the curves so that there are no unsightly bulges of fabric. Allow to dry.
7. Upholster the cushions in the same manner.
8. Glue the back to the seat as shown in the plans.
9. Glue the cushions in place.
10. Glue the leg assemblies to the sides of the sofa.

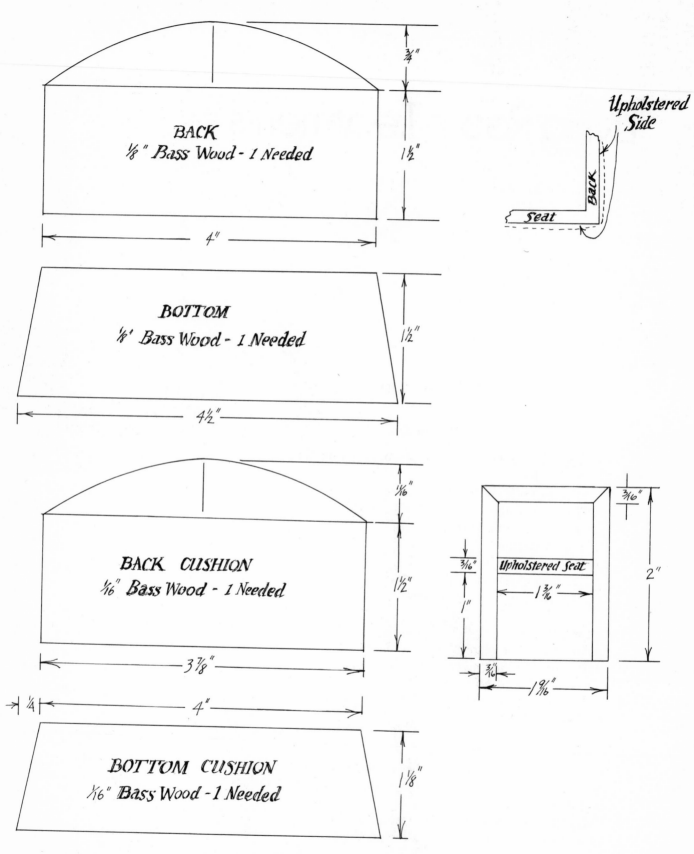

BACK
⅛" Bass Wood - 1 Needed

Upholstered Side

Seat   Back

¾"

1½"

4"

BOTTOM
⅛' Bass Wood - 1 Needed

1½"

4½"

BACK CUSHION
1/16" Bass Wood - 1 Needed

1/16"

1½"

3 ⅞"

Upholstered Seat

3/16"

3/16"

1"

1 3/16"

2"

3/16"

1 9/16"

¼

4"

BOTTOM CUSHION
1/16" Bass Wood - 1 Needed

1⅛"

HALL SETTEE

24

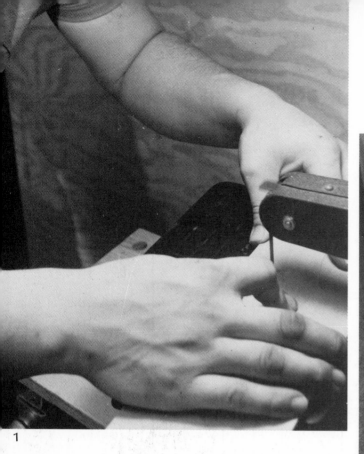

1

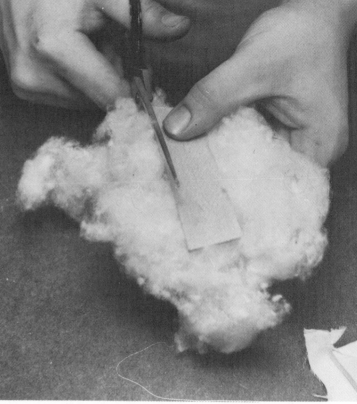

2

Hall settee how-to steps by Frederick Decker.

3

(See finished settee, page 29.)

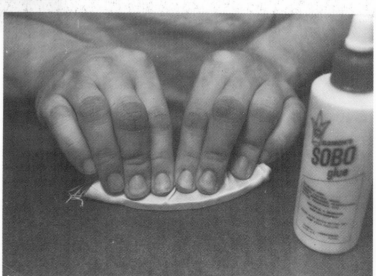

4

WING CHAIR

Materials

Cardboard backing for cushions
Sobo glue
X-acto knife
Jeweler's saw or power scroll saw
Scissors
Pencil
1 sheet of basswood, ⅛″, for frame
1 piece of mahogany, ⅛″ × 2″, for legs
¼″ foam rubber or polyester fiber filling for
  padding

1. Cut out the back, sides, and bottom with a jeweler's saw or power scroll saw. When cutting out the sides tape the two pieces together with double-faced tape to get the contours exactly the same.

2. Cut out the back cushion, two side cushions, and seat cushion from medium-weight card stock, again taping together two pieces of stock for the sides, as you did with the basswood.

3. Now comes a more complicated step. Lay out the three cut-out basswood pieces as shown in the plans. As you can see, the corners where the sides and back meet stick out a bit and do not join properly. Take your X-acto knife and trim the corners down so they meet properly. At this time it is a good idea to label the pieces right, left, inside, and outside.

4. Lay the back piece on your fabric and mark out a section ½″ larger on all sides. You will need two of these: one for the back and one for the back cushion. Do the same for the bottom.

5. To cut out the upholstery for the side pieces, take a piece of fabric 4″ × 12″ and fold it with the back side showing, so you have a rectangle 4″ × 6″. Lay the left side piece of basswood down on it. Draw out your pattern ½″ larger, and cut as you did for the back and side, and label each piece as to which is left outside and left cushion. Do the same for the right side.

6. Now you are ready to start gluing the fabric to the wood pieces. Start with the simplest part—the bottom. Put a small line of Sobo and attach the fabric and allow to dry. Fold the fabric over the bottom and glue to the opposite edge. Repeat on the other sides in the same manner, mitering the corners so there are no unsightly bulges of fabric. Next do the back piece. Remember two points: (a) it is the outside of the sides

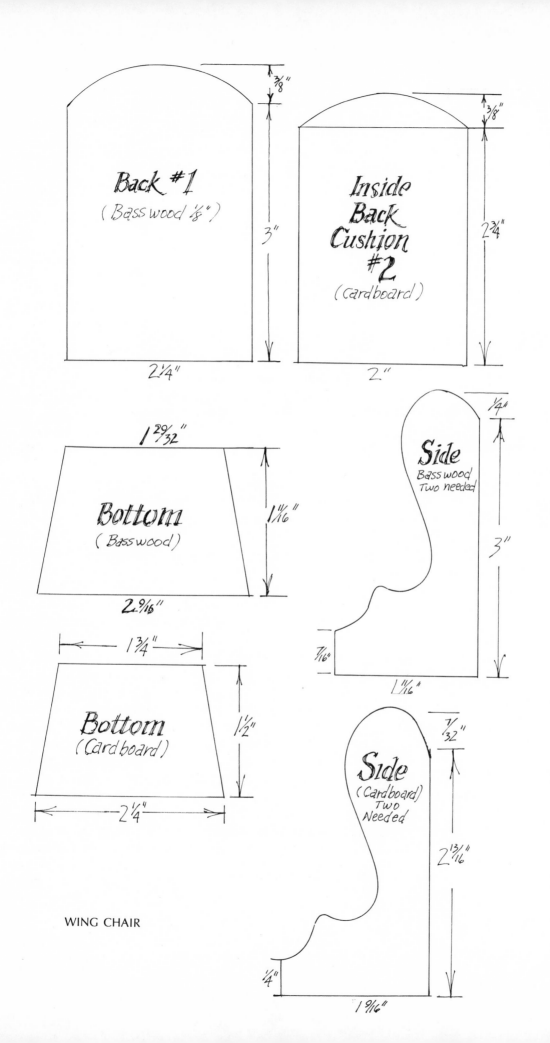

Back #1
(Basswood ⅛")

3"

2¼"

Inside
Back
Cushion
#2
(cardboard)

3/8"

2¾"

2"

1²⁹⁄₃₂"

Bottom
(Basswood)

1¹¹⁄₁₆"

2⁹⁄₁₆"

Side
Basswood
Two needed

¼"

3"

⁷⁄₁₆"

1¹¹⁄₁₆"

1¾"

Bottom
(Cardboard)

1½"

2¼"

Side
(Cardboard)
Two
Needed

⁷⁄₃₂"

2¹³⁄₁₆"

¼"

1⁹⁄₁₆"

WING CHAIR

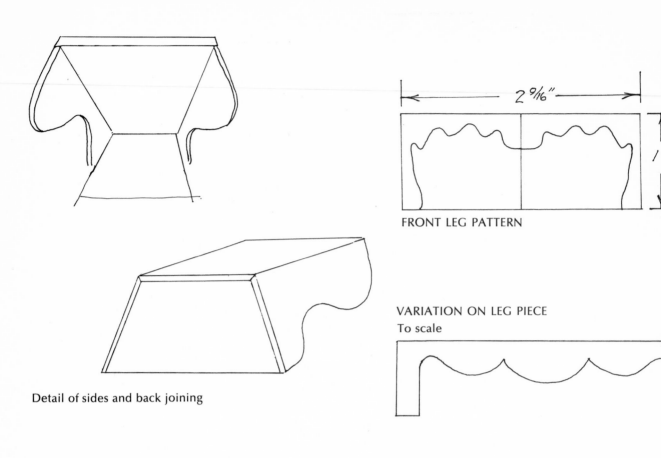

2 9/16″

1″

FRONT LEG PATTERN

Detail of sides and back joining

VARIATION ON LEG PIECE
To scale

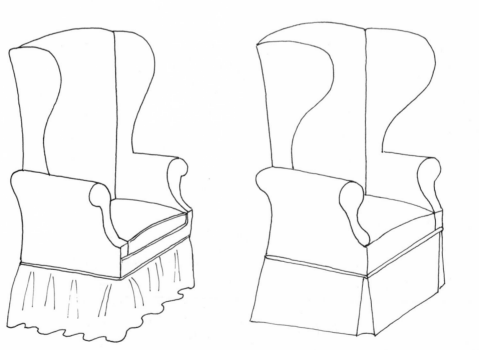

WING CHAIR VARIATIONS

and back that are covered with fabric; (b) when upholstering pieces with curves it is much easier to do the straight sides first, leaving the sides with curves till last. When doing the curves, work on only a small section of the curve at a time, mitering the fabric as you go, so that there are no bulges in the material.

7. While the wood pieces are drying you can glue the padding to the cardboard pieces, taking care to glue the padding to the inside of the two side pieces. Allow to dry.

8. Take the bottom piece, upholstered side down, and glue the chair sides to it, upholstered sides out, and allow to dry.

9. Trim padding on the cardboard pieces to its proper size and cover them as you did the pieces of basswood. Allow to dry.

10. Glue back cushion to uncovered side of chair back and glue this piece to the bottom and side assembly.

11. Glue side cushions to inside of chair.

12. Glue bottom cushion to chair.

13. Trace pattern for front legs onto a piece of $\frac{1}{8}'' \times 2''$ mahogany, cut it out and glue flush to the front of the chair.

14. Cut one mahogany strip $\frac{1}{8}'' \times \frac{1}{4}'' \times 2''$ and glue to the back of the chair.

Hall settee with plans by Frederick Decker.

Terry Rogal teaching beginning furniture making at Mini Mundus school.

Victorian wing chair by Terry Rogal.

15. Cut two mahogany strips $\frac{1}{8}" \times \frac{1}{4}" \times 2\frac{11}{16}"$ and glue to the sides of the chair. N.B.: Here a little work with your X-acto knife may be necessary to get the pieces to fit flush with the sides.

16. Cut two legs out of mahogany $\frac{1}{8}" \times \frac{1}{8}" \times 1"$ and glue to the inside of the corners at the back of the chair, and you are done.

17. If you wish to put a kick pleat or a dust ruffle on the chair, steps 13 through 16 may be eliminated. You can substitute four pieces of basswood $\frac{1}{8}" \times \frac{1}{8}" \times 1"$ for the legs and attach the dust ruffle or kick pleat. Also you may prefer to decrease the strip sizes given in steps 14 and 15 so that the rear legs can be placed on the extreme rear corners of the chair.

LAWSON SOFA

Materials

1 piece of $\frac{1}{2}"$ pine lumber, $6\frac{1}{2}" \times \frac{3}{4}"$
1 piece of $\frac{1}{2}"$ pine lumber, $6\frac{1}{2}" \times 1\frac{1}{2}"$
1 piece of $\frac{1}{4}"$ pine lumber, $\frac{3}{4}" \times 6\frac{1}{2}"$
2 pieces of $\frac{1}{4}"$ pine lumber, $1\frac{3}{4}" \times 2\frac{1}{4}"$
1 piece of $\frac{1}{4}"$ pine lumber, $1\frac{3}{4}" \times 6"$
  Sobo glue
  Hacksaw or jeweler's saw
  Panel nails
  Cotton batting

Fabric

1 piece, $9\frac{1}{2}" \times 5"$, for base
1 piece, $6\frac{1}{2}" \times 7\frac{1}{2}"$, for base
2 pieces, $6\frac{1}{2}" \times 6"$, for sides
1 piece, $6\frac{1}{2}" \times 3"$, for seat cushion
2 pieces, $\frac{3}{4}" \times 7"$, for under base
2 pieces, $\frac{3}{4}" \times 4"$, for legs
1 piece, $32"$, for welting

1. Using $\frac{1}{2}"$ pine lumber, cut out one strip, $6\frac{1}{2}" \times \frac{3}{4}"$. Take the strip and cut out three legs $\frac{1}{4}" \times \frac{1}{2}"$, one at each end and one in the center (see illustration 26-a).

2. Cut a second piece of $\frac{1}{2}"$ pine lumber, $6\frac{1}{2}" \times 1\frac{1}{2}"$. This is the base of the sofa. On one side, glue the pine strip with the three cut-out legs. This becomes the front of the sofa. Allow glue to dry.

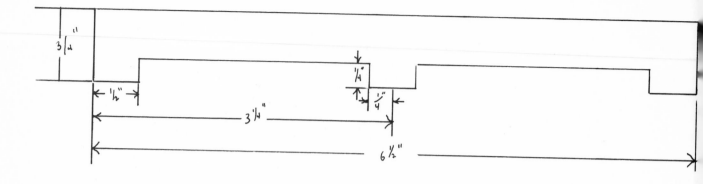

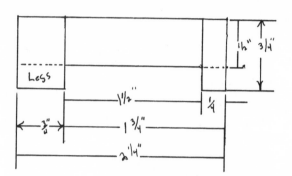

LAWSON SOFA

3. Using ¼″ pine lumber, cut one piece ¾″ × 6½″. This becomes the back support leg. Glue this piece to the opposite side of the 6½″ × 1½″ strip (see illustration 26-b).

4. Taking a ¼″ pine strip, cut the arms and the back. Cut two pieces of 1¾″ × 2¼″, and one piece 1¾″ × 6″. Arms will be at each side and the back will fit between the arms.

5. Cover the base first. Slit fabric at corners in order to cover around the legs. Glue fabric to underneath side of the base.

6. Cover front of back piece with cotton batting. Working from the bottom up, glue or staple the fabric at the bottom. Work it up over the front, top, and back. (Don't fasten back.)

7. Do the same at the sides. Cover sides first with the cotton batting. Then, with fabric, cover the bottom, work it up over the front (seat side), top, and back. When material on the inside is taut and pulled around to corners, place arms and back on the base. Make sure all the fabric on the inside corners is tucked inside. Place it carefully where it belongs. Using panel nails, nail arms and back in place from the bottom. Use as few nails as possible to secure.

8. When secured, complete the wrapping of the fabric around the arms and the back. Fold edges of the front arms around to the sides. Fold edges in ¼″ and glue. Glue all the way down to the bottom of the legs.

9. Complete wrapping the back. Tuck it into the arm sides, ¼″ edge folded under and glued. Glue all the way down and over the legs.

Lawson sofa by Lynn Kusnet.

10. Cut two strips of the same fabric, ¾″ × 7″. Fold it under ¼″. Make two shorter strips, ¾″ × 4″. Fold to measure ¼″ wide.
11. Use shorter pieces to cover sides. This gives the legs a finished look.
12. Cambric or lining material can be cut to cover up the raw wood on the bottom.
13. For welting, measure seat, 6″ across and 2″ wide. Make welting to cover four times as much.
14. Use upholsterer's thread, or thin nylon cord, which is thicker than sewing thread.
15. Cut out two pieces of fabric for the cushion, ½″ longer or ½″ wider, with ½″ between bottom and top. Sew it on the wrong side, leaving one end open. Fill with cotton batting. Turn right side out. Sew remaining end.

It is a little difficult working on this small scale upholstering, so work slowly and have patience! You will find that the fabric dimensions give a little extra salvage and you will have ample fabric for working.

GRECO-ROMAN RECLINING COUCH

Materials

2 pieces of basswood, if you plan to paint, or a small-grained hardwood, if you plan to stain, 2″ × ⅛″ × 22″

2 pieces of basswood strip dowel, ⅛″ × 1⅝″
Cardboard thin enough to bend easily for patterns
Cotton batting for back, seat, arms

2 pieces of basswood strip, ⅛″ × 1⅝″
Transparent glue such as Elmer's (Sobo for fabric edges) for joining
Paint, enamel, or stain and varnish
Fabric in scale. Enough to cover back, seat, arms, and the outside back and arms with 1″ extra on each piece. Dorothy Wade used a Scalamandre Roman stripe (approximately $40 a yard!), 12″ long and 8″ wide, and had ample fabric

½ yard 1⁄16″ decorative cord (optional)

1. Cut and glue bottom and seat with back against seat on the outside.
2. Cut, sand, and stain or size all other pieces. Sand, clean, and apply varnish or enamel or paint. Choose a color to complement or harmonize with the fabric.
3. Cover back with glue and apply ½″ thickness of cotton evenly. Allow to dry.
4. Trace cardboard pattern onto fabric with ½″ of fabric extending beyond cardboard all around.
5. Stretch fabric evenly, observing with care that woof and warp are absolutely vertical and horizontal. Stretch fabric over edges of back piece and secure temporarily with masking tape only on the rear of back piece. Glue lower excess fabric to back edge of seat. Dry.
6. Glue cardboard strips #IX to front trim pieces.
7. Paste cotton to side arm pieces of cardboard and bend to shape to accommodate shapes of back edges and cardboard strips on front trims.

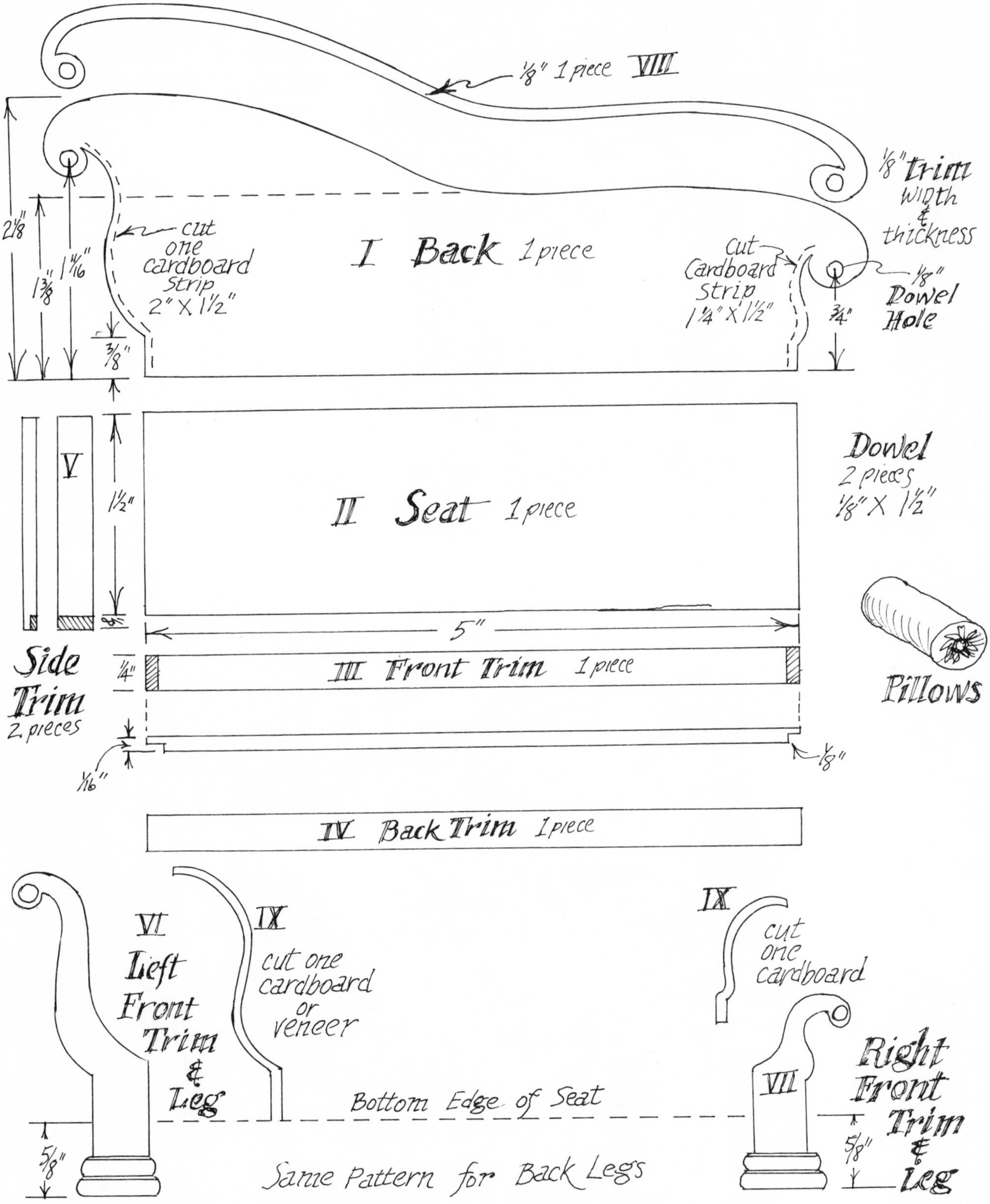

1/8" 1 piece VIII
1/8" Trim width & thickness
cut one cardboard strip 2" X 1 1/2"
I Back 1 piece
cut cardboard strip 1 1/4" X 1 1/2"
1/8" Dowel Hole
2 1/8"
1 3/8"
1 11/16"
3/8"
3/4"
V
1 1/2"
II Seat 1 piece
Dowel 2 pieces 1/8" X 1 1/2"
5"
1/4"
III Front Trim 1 piece
Side Trim 2 pieces
Pillows
1/16"
1/8"
IV Back Trim 1 piece
VI Left Front Trim & Leg
IX cut one cardboard or veneer
IX cut one cardboard
VII
Right Front Trim & Leg
Bottom Edge of Seat
5/8"
5/8"
Same Pattern for Back Legs

GRECO-ROMAN RECLINING COUCH

Close-up of the Woodcraft finger plane. Made of brass and walnut with steel cutting blade.

Greco-Roman reclining couch by Dorothy Wade. Made of red mahogany wood and striped silk fabric.

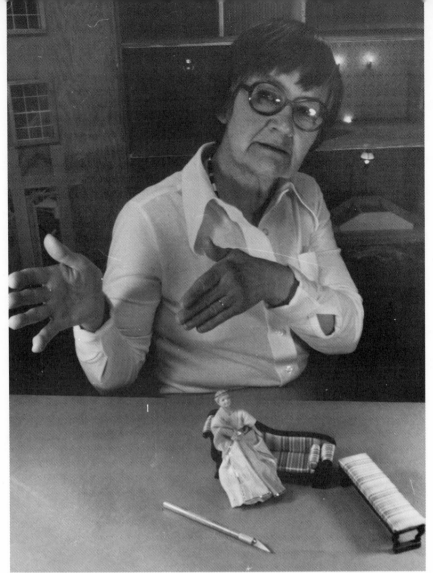

Dorothy Wade, creator of the Greco-Roman reclining couch and bench.

8. Glue cardboard arm pieces onto dowels with edge of cardboard feathered to a fine edge. These are upper edges of strips. When dry, place top edge of arm fabric on same edge of left dowel and glue in place. When dry, wind counterclockwise enough to hide edge of cardboard and fabric.

9. Repeat same procedure with right arm, winding clockwise. Allow to dry.

10. Glue front seat trim piece to leg pieces. Allow to dry.

11. Glue dowel ends into front arm trim with glued edges of cardboard fabric rolled underneath. Dry.

12. Glue left and right trim to side arm fabric-covered cardboard pieces which are glued to cardboard strips; secure with tape on outside edges.

13. Glue lower edge of excess fabric to left and right sides of seat. Glue in place. Dry.

14. Glue top back trim to edge of couch back. Dry.

15. Glue dowels into dowel holes.
16. Cover outside of couch body with fabric.
17. Trim top edge in back with ¹⁄₁₆″ cord to cover glued edge of backing of fabric.
18. Glue lower back trim to lower back edge and the two side trims. At this time, glue side trim pieces to front leg trim pieces.
19. Glue back legs to back trim piece on inside abutting side pieces.
20. Make seat cushions by cutting one piece of cardboard to fit seat. Glue cotton to depth of ¼″ and cover with fabric. Glue bottom side onto seat.
21. Round pillows ½″ × ¼″. Glue fabric to round, sausage-shaped rolls of cotton.

GRECO-ROMAN BENCH

Materials

1 piece of basswood, if you plan to paint, or hardwood if you plan to stain, 2″ × ³⁄₁₆″ × 12″
Cardboard for patterns for pedestals
8 straight pins
White glue or epoxy
1 piece of foam rubber, 1½″ × ³⁄₁₆″ × 12″
1 piece of fabric, 2³⁄₈″ × 6³⁄₈″

1. Cut out the seat and the two end pieces for the bases.
2. Cut out and carve the four pedestals using the pattern traced onto cardboard. The top should be slightly wider than the base.
3. Drill holes as per diagrams 1 and 4, to go through seat and bases but to penetrate only about halfway into the back ends of each pedestal.
4. Sand, clean, and stain each piece, or give the wood a primer coat if you plan to paint.
5. Sand all the pieces lightly with the finest grade of sandpaper or steel wool.
6. Clean and apply second coat of stain or paint. Allow to dry. At this time you can either varnish or wax the pieces. Where the edges are to be glued, clean off the wax and varnish and allow to dry.
7. Cut the ends off the pins so that the heads will be slightly countersunk into the holes.

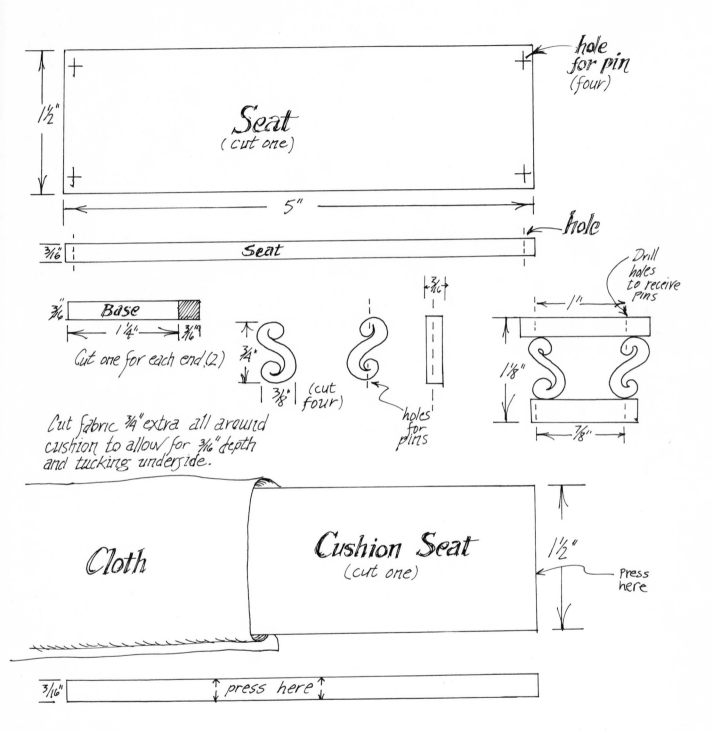

Seat
(cut one)

hole
for pin
(four)

1½"

5"

³⁄₁₆"

Seat

hole

³⁄₁₆" Base

1¼"   ³⁄₁₆"

Cut one for each end.(2)

¾"

³⁄₈" (cut four)

holes for pins

³⁄₁₆"

Drill holes to receive pins

1"

1⅛"

⅞"

Cut fabric ¾" extra all around cushion to allow for ³⁄₁₆" depth and tucking underside.

Cloth

Cushion Seat
(cut one)

1½"

Press here

³⁄₁₆"

press here

GRECO-ROMAN BENCH

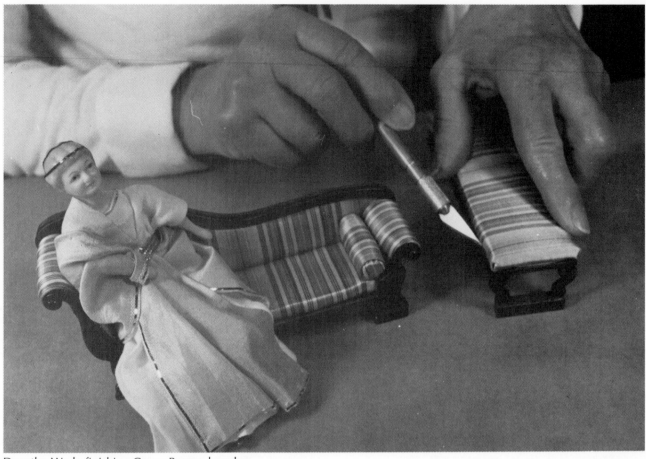
Dorothy Wade finishing Greco-Roman bench.

8. Apply the glue to all the pins and pieces and assemble. Allow to dry.
9. Assemble pedestals to top piece first and allow to dry.
10. Assemble pedestals to the base pieces and allow to dry.
11. Press edges along fabric so that a neat square edge will exactly fit the foam rubber.
12. Apply fabric to foam by squaring each corner and securing beneath.
13. Glue the completed cushion to the seat.

VICTORIAN TUFTED SOFA

Materials

2 pieces softwood (bass or balsa), 5⅜″ × 1¾″, for seat

2 pieces cardboard, 4″ × 8½″, soft and thin enough to bend easily but stiff enough to remain rigid

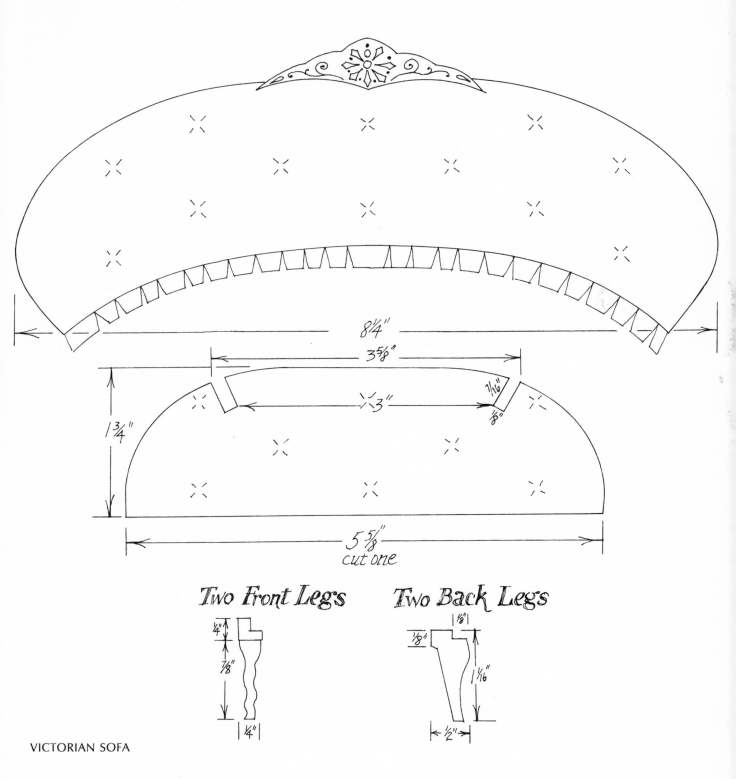

8¼"

3⅝"

7/16"

3"

⅛"

1¾"

5⅝"
cut one

Two Front Legs

¼"

⅛"

¼"

Two Back Legs

⅛"

⅛"

1 1/16"

½"

VICTORIAN SOFA

41

1 piece hardwood, small-grained such as walnut, mahogany, or cherry, 1″ × 8″ × ⅛″

1 length of basket-weave round rush, ⅛″ × 12″

1 piece polyester filling, 4″ × 10″ × ½″ or more, for upholstery padding

Fabric, design in scale, silk or cotton or panne velvet, color to harmonize with the wood, stain, or paint

1 skein D.M.C. cotton perle crochet floss for trim border

Stain or paint of your choice

Varnish or wax

White drying glue such as Sobo

4 straight pins

1. Cut bottom piece of wood.
2. Cut and carve front legs and back legs. Sand, clean off, and stain. Dry.
3. At same time sand, clean, and stain the basket-weave rush. Dry.
4. Cut cardboard pattern for back of sofa, seat, and decorative piece on top center of sofa. Trace carved pattern onto wood, cut to shape and size, and carve.
5. Sand, clean, and stain the decorative piece when you are staining #2 and #3. Dry.
6. Rule lines on back and seat cardboard pieces for the placement of tufting marks as per drawing. If you wish closer tufting, adjust pattern.
7. Punch needle-sized holes through cardboard at tufting marks.
8. Spread glue on cardboard after shaping back piece of cardboard to conform to curve. On back and seat, place polyester fiber about ¾″ to 1″ thick. Dry.
9. Cut fabric from cardboard pattern, allowing at least ¾″ all around to compensate for tufting.
10. Lay fabric on polyester and catch at center with running thread, vertical and horizontal, being careful to keep design of material on the square.
11. Thread embroidery needle with cotton floss. Work from cardboard back, thrust needle and thread through center hole, then through fabric make a 4-turn French knot, return needle and thread through same hole but with enough cardboard between entry and reentry to allow you to tie a knot. Go to next hole and repeat the same process as you go until tufting is completed.
12. Apply a covering of masking tape over complete back to cover knotting and make a firmer back.

Victorian sofa and chair by Dorothy Wade; Victoriana dolls by Vicky New-house. Photograph by Peter Schaaf.

13. Glue tufted seat to bottom wooden piece. Clamp with wooden strips or boards. Dry.
14. Glue legs to wooden piece, dry. Drill holes in seat and legs for cut-off piece of pine for strength.
15. Glue back to seat, with bottom edge meeting bottom edge of seat. Glue and then glue tabs, along bottom curve under slat.
16. Pull excess fabric of seat under seat and glue, securing with tape while drying.
17. Cover complete back with fabric and pull excess lower edge under seat.
18. Cover under seat neatly with cardboard or inexpensive strong fabric.
19. Glue decorative piece in place. Dry.
20. With cotton floss crochet a chain stitch long enough to use as border to go around back seat and around leg joinings and top of back side of back.
21. Glue the piece of basket-weave rush around top edge of back sofa, beginning where front legs join sofa, up and around to spot where decorative piece joins sofa at outer ends. Hold in place by overcast stitch with strong white thread where piece is dry and secure. Snip threads so they won't show.
22. With Sobo carefully glue the chain stitch trim to cover glue marks along inside edges of rush back and front. Keep in place with sequin pins until dry.

The Americana Miniatures Kit is precut and all the materials, including glue and sandpaper, are included. Excellent quality hardwood is used.

If you prefer to start from scratch, a similar style has been designed.

CLASSIC SOFA AND CHAIR

Materials

1 sheet basswood, ⅛″ × 3″
1 strip basswood, ⅛″ × ³⁄₁₆″
1 strip basswood, ½″ × 2″
1 scrap ⅜″ plywood (from a dollhouse)
White glue such as Sobo
1 piece of fabric, 12″ × 18″
Stain
Jigsaw

1. Cut the back cushion, back, and seat cushion out of ⅛″ basswood.
2. Cut the bottom from a scrap of ⅜″ plywood, taking care to angle the back edge as shown in the plans.
3. Cut the legs out of the ⅛″ × ³⁄₁₆″ basswood and stain.
4. Trace the pattern of the left side onto a piece of ½″ basswood and shape. A good idea here is to cut a template for the arm shape so you can check your progress properly. Reverse the template and do the right arm in the same manner.
5. Cut out the arms from the shaped pieces, using the dimensions given in the plans.
6. Glue the padding to the back cushion and seat cushion; set aside and allow to dry.
7. Upholster the bottom side of the bottom piece and one side of the back piece.
8. Glue the legs to the arm pieces and upholster these pieces so that the only wood showing is the legs.
9. Upholster the cushions, mitering the corners and curves to eliminate bulges in the fabric.
10. Glue the back cushion to the bare side of the back piece.
11. Using ½″ brads, nail the back and sides to the bottom, clipping off the nailheads so they do not show.

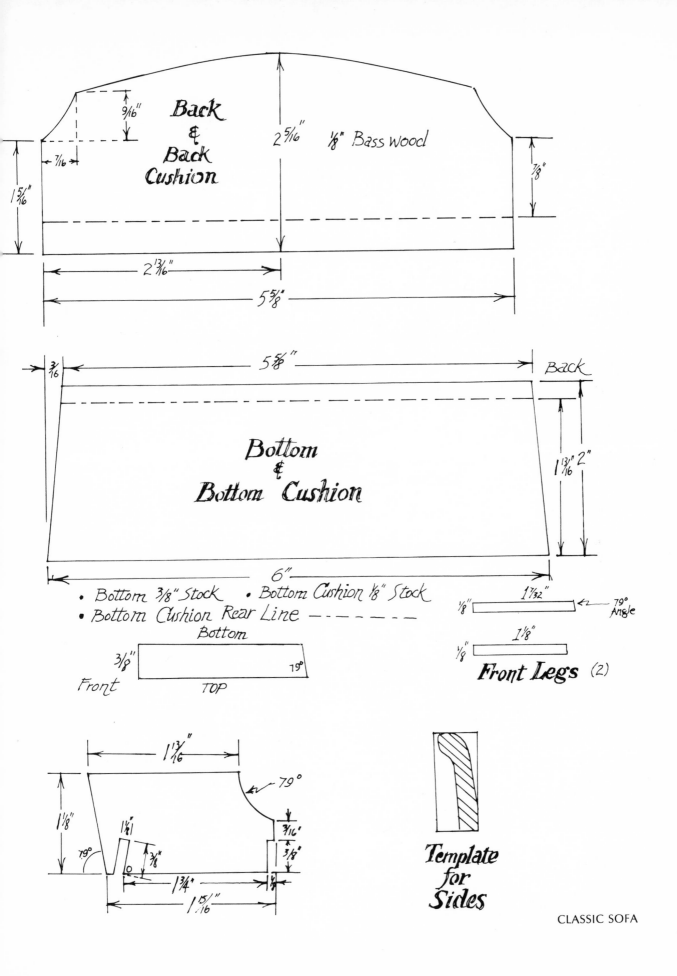

Back
&
Back
Cushion

9/16"

7/16"

1 5/16"

2 5/16"   1/8" Bass wood

7/8"

2 13/16"

5 5/8"

3/16"

5 5/8"   Back

1 13/16" 2"

Bottom
&
Bottom Cushion

6"

• Bottom 3/8" Stock   • Bottom Cushion 1/8" Stock
• Bottom Cushion Rear Line — — — —

Bottom

3/8"   79°
Front   TOP

1 7/32"   79°
1/8"   Angle

1 1/8"
1/8"   Front Legs (2)

1 13/16"

79°

1 1/8"

79°

1 1/4"

3/16"

3/8"

1 1/4"

3/8"

1 3/4"

1 5/16"

Template
for
Sides

CLASSIC SOFA

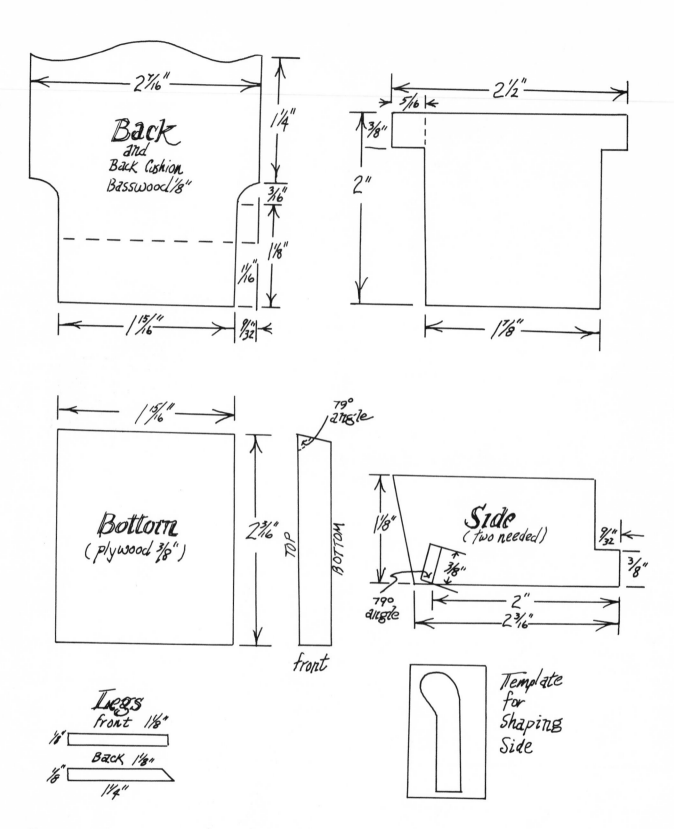

Back
and
Back Cushion
Basswood 1/8"

2 7/16"

1 1/4"

3/16"

1 1/8"

11/16"

1 15/16"

9/32"

2 1/2"

5/16"

3/8"

2"

1 7/8"

Bottom
(plywood 3/8")

1 15/16"

2 3/16"

TOP

BOTTOM

front

79°
angle

Side
(two needed)

1 1/8"

3/8"

79°
angle

2"

2 3/16"

9/32"

3/8"

Legs
front 1 1/8"

1/8"

Back 1 1/8"

1/8"

1 1/4"

Template
for
Shaping
Side

CLASSIC CHAIR

Upholstered chair by Americana Miniatures.

Upholstered chair kit by Americana Miniatures.

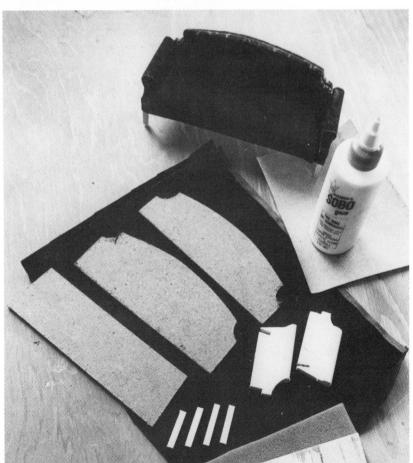

Upholstered sofa by Americana Miniatures.

LIVING ROOM KITS

If you are making petit point or bargello cushions, or covering a seat cushion with an antique fabric, these Queen Anne pieces are in keeping with the craftsmanship of your fabric.

Masterpiece Miniatures are perfect if you don't want to spend several hundred dollars per chair for a Queen Anne chair and settee. These pieces are precision-reproduced in fine metal, enabling collectors to add magnificently excellent pieces to their collections at comparatively low prices. They are available in very easily assembled kit form, accompanied by finishing instructions that will enable you to obtain museum-quality finishes, wood grain and all. Unless one handles these kits, no one will know they are not made of wood.

Queen Anne side chair, Philadelphia, circa 1750–1760
    Height: 3½" Width: 2"   Kit: $12
Queen Anne armchair   Kit: $14
Queen Anne double settee
    Height: 3½" Width: 4½"   Kit: $20
Chippendale tassel-back chair, Philadelphia, circa 1750–1780
    Height: 3¾" Width: 2"   Kit: $12
Chippendale tassel-back armchair   Kit: $14
Chippendale tassel-back settee   Kit: $20

Accompanying pieces include highboys, lowboys, pedestal dining room table, side table, piecrust table, tea table, and corner table.

Realife Scientific Models offers a complete room setting for $15.95. The upholstered chair in the library and the sofa in the music room are very attractive pieces. The piano makes up beautifully.

The X-acto Kits feature a graceful Federal sofa and wing chair. At the moment the fabric is a plain blue but you may want to substitute your own fabric. They have perfect Chippendale chairs and settee.

Lillie Putt colonial living room kits require some sewing. No wood is showing. All pieces have a ruffled hem at the bottom.

The Colvin Kits are easy to make. They require only gluing. Highly recommended for children to make. See the wing chair holding Jimmy Carter in the "Inhabitants" chapter.

Masterpiece Miniatures kit.

Masterpiece Miniatures kit.

Realife living room kit.

Realife library kit.

Realife music room kit.

Jacobean crewel living room drapery, valances and upholstery for wing chair
and loveseat on linen. A kit from Create Your Own.

3
Bedroom Treatments

FOUR-POSTER BED

Materials

2 pieces ⅞″ × ¼″ basswood cut 5¾″ long (side pieces *A*)

2 pieces ⅞″ × ¼″ basswood cut 3¾″ long (front and back pieces *B*)

4 pieces ³⁄₁₆″ × ³⁄₁₆″ basswood cut ⅞″ long (supports *C*)

1 piece ⅛″ basswood cut 3¾″ × 1½″ (headboard, which will be cut according to pattern *D*)

4 ¼″ dowels cut 7″ long (bedposts *E*)

Heavy cotton string

1. Start with pieces *A* and *B* and drill holes approximately ³⁄₃₂″ in diameter. There will be seven holes ¾″ apart in *A* pieces and five holes ⅝″ apart in *B* pieces. All holes should be ¼″ up from edge.
2. Cut headboard (*D*) according to pattern given with jeweler's saw or jigsaw.
3. Shape bedposts (*E*) with miniature lathe or small files and sandpaper according to pattern given.
4. Sand all pieces well, finishing with wet/dry sandpaper.
5. Glue pieces together following diagram.

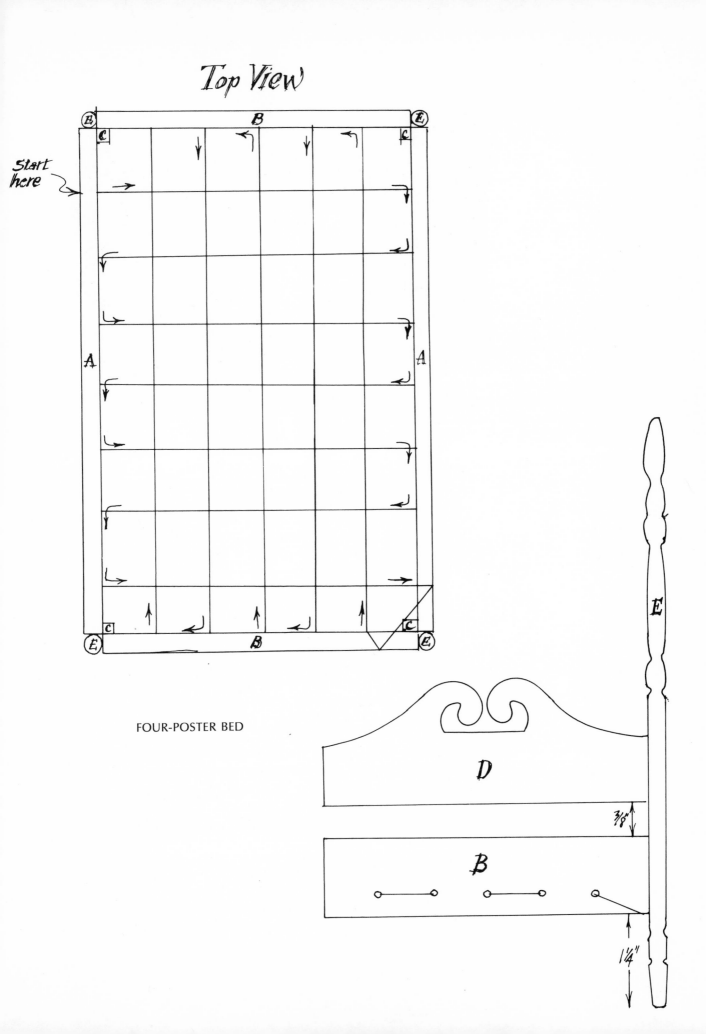

Top View

Start here

B

C · C

A · A

C · C

B

FOUR-POSTER BED

E

D

3/8"

B

1¼"

Four-poster bed (underside view). Reproduced by Terry Rogal.

MATTRESS

The mattress is made from ticking cotton stuffed with loose batting. The dimensions given are for a 4″ × 6″ four-poster bed.

1. Cut two pieces of ticking, 4″ × 6″.
2. Cut one piece of ticking 1″ × 15½″.
3. Sew strip around four sides of one rectangle and three sides of the other, leaving a short end open for stuffing. Turn fabric, stuff, and slip-stitch closed.

GINGHAM QUILT

Materials

¼ yard or 8½″ × 10½″ pieces of 1″ check gingham
Thin layer of polyester batting, pink batting, pink batiste lining (hand-quilted in pink)

1. Measure bed to determine size in whole inches. Measure across the top and down both sides. Notch the corners squarely, if necessary or desired, and cut gingham and lining to size, leaving

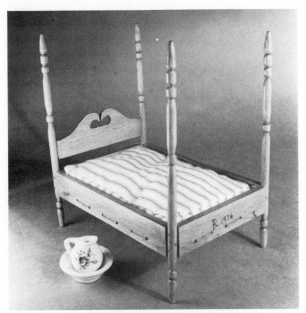

Four-poster bed with mattress.

Four-poster bed with gingham quilt. Original creation by Theresa Klink.

¼" seam allowance all around. With gingham side up, stitch around seam line, leaving one side open for turning and stuffing.

2. Lay batting over quilt and baste to seam line. Clip and notch batting close to basting line, turn, poke out corners, and press seams flat. (The quilt can also be stuffed with loose batting. Turn, poke, and press the quilt material right side out and press seams flat. Now carefully lay pieces of stuffing inside, putting much less on the sides than on the top.)

3. Slip-stitch the open side closed, pinning as necessary to hold the batting in place; quilt with a single thread of regular sewing thread, starting from the center and working to the outside.

4. The pillow is gingham on both sides, approximately 2" × 4" in size. Matching the checks, sew around three sides, leaving the short side open. Turn and poke and press as you did with the quilt. Stuff with batting and then slip-stitch closed. Tiny ¼"-wide braid is then sewn around the top edge. If desired, the pillow can also have a quilted effect. To do this, simply use a small running stitch and follow the line of the checks in the gingham.

Canopy bed by Donald Dube; hook rug by Margaret Dilley.

DUST RUFFLE

The dust ruffle is made of the same material as the quilt lining. Cut a strip 4″ × 34″. Flat-fell the seam ends together. Press edges of loop ¼″ on both sides. Turn one edge up 1″ for bottom hem, and machine stitch all the way around the bottom hem. Turn the other edge in ¼″, and machine stitch around, leaving ½″ open. Tie one end of an elastic braid 16″ long to a bobby pin. Feed the braid through the casing, taking care not to lose the other end. Join the other ends in a square knot and stitch the casing closed.

Flat-fell seam: a method of finishing so that you cannot see the raw edges, as followed by the French couturieres. The Vogue Sewing book describes this technique which is very complicated but very beautiful.

56

SWEETHEART BLOSSOM APPLIQUÉD QUILT

This quilt is hand-appliquéd, in two or more parts, on white batiste, cotton sheath lining, or any other semitransparent, white, or pale-colored material. The fabric for appliqué should be very fine, lightweight, closely woven cotton prints or solids. Cotton lawn is perfect if you can find it.

Decide what size to make your quilt. Squares of quilt are 2″ × 2″. Sixteen squares make a quilt 8″ × 8″. This quilt is fourteen squares, 8″ × 8″, with bottom and corner squares notched out.

1. Cut a square of the face material 12″ × 12″. Fasten the square over the pattern in the book, centering the square of fabric over the center of the pattern, making sure that the lines in the fabric run parallel with the lines on the graph. Trace the pattern onto the fabric then lift the fabric, turning it 180 degrees, mating the center edge, and transferring the pattern to the other half.

Sweetheart blossom appliquéd quilt by Bonnie McLean; brass bed from Clare-Bell Brassworks.

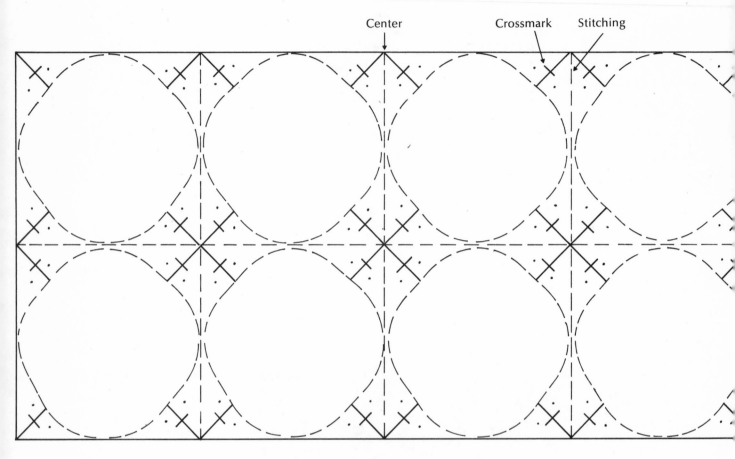

Center   Crossmark   Stitching

SWEETHEART BLOSSOM APPLIQUÉD QUILT

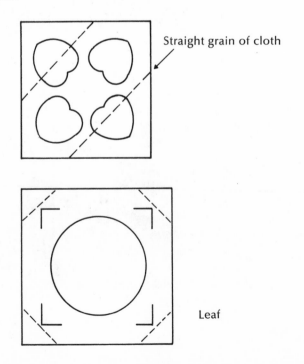

Straight grain of cloth

Leaf

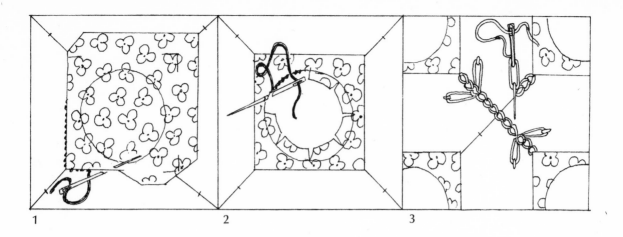

1   2   3

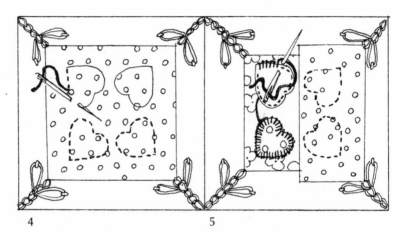

4   5

SWEETHEART BLOSSOM APPLIQUÉD QUILT STITCHES

2. Cut out the leaf and heart templates in cardboard or hard paper. With pointed X-acto knife carefully cut out a hole in the leaf template and the hearts in the heart template. Cut as many squares as you need of the leaf template in green print. Place leaf template on fabric, align the template with the grain of the fabric, and trace pattern onto it. Do not cut out hole in fabric until after the square has been sewn down onto the face of the quilt. Diagram 1: Lay square of green over markings on quilt face (between the X's), matching the corners of the square to the small cross marks on the solid lines. Use a hoop when sewing the square to quilt face.

3. Turn in the edge ³⁄₁₆″ and blindstitch around the outside edge, clipping or folding in the corners as you go. Using one strand of cotton floss, blindstitch, keeping the edge of the square on the straight grain of fabric. Diagram 2: Carefully nip into the center of the circle in the leaf square, and not into the quilt face. Cut out a circle ³⁄₁₆″ smaller than the circle on the leaf square. Clip to the line on straight and bias grains. Turn fabric under to line, one segment at a time, and blindstitch down.

4. Diagram 3: With two strands of green floss, starting from the corner of the square, make three short chain stitches to the cross mark. Make two lazy daisy stitches in third chain stitch, running them parallel to square, then work six more chain stitches to the next cross mark, repeat the two lazy daisy stitches, and finish off with three more chain stitches. Cut as many sets of hearts as needed, making sure to cut them on the bias as shown on the template. With sharp pencil, carefully mark outlines of hearts through template. Arrange the square with four hearts over square with circle. Pin square down with fine needles. With one strand of floss, make tiny running stitches around each heart. Split fabric between hearts and one at a time cut out hearts close around running stitches. Using a buttonhole stitch, stitch over the running stitches around the heart, with one strand of floss and a tiny needle. Press quilt face down over soft velour towel.
5. This quilt is stuffed with a piece of sweat shirt, fuzzy side up. Sweat shirt material is soft and heavy enough to allow sides to hang. Cotton flannel or batting can also be used. Cut lining and batting to approximate size of quilt face.
6. Lay quilt face over pattern in book and with sharp pencil carefully work over dashed lines, which are quilting lines, with tiny dots every ⅜″ or ½″.
7. Lay batting out, lay quilt face over stuffing face up; lay lining fabric over this and stitch around three sides, leaving a short side open for turning. This step attaches the batting to the quilt. Clip corners and trim batting close to seam line. Turn and poke out corners, then slip-stitch opening.
8. Quilt by hand or machine along dotted lines, starting from the center, quilting the straight lines first.

GEOMETRIC STAR APPLIQUÉD QUILT

This quilt is all hand-appliquéd. Four print fabrics are used —one forming the base to which the other pieces are appliquéd.

1. Using transfer crayons or pencils (light-colored pencils if you use a dark-base fabric), go over the lines on the pattern and transfer to the face of a 9″ square of the base fabric. If you don't wish to tear the page from the book, trace it onto a piece of thin white paper with the transfer pencil or crayon. If the printed diagram can be the only help to you, transfer the 4″ × 2″ half diagram to a sheet of white paper, laying the center of the paper over the center line of the diagram. Turn the paper around (180°) and repeat. This gives a complete transfer pattern.

Geometric star appliquéd quilt by Bonnie McLean.

2. Cut four of the **V**-shaped pieces from the second fabric. Cut eight of the trapezoids from the third fabric. Cut four 1″ × 7″ strips from the fourth fabric. Cut two squares from the template—one each from the third and fourth fabrics. Transfer the trapezoid shapes from the template to the square of the fourth fabric. Either transfer with transfer pencils or cut the template and stencil onto the fabric. Cut a 1″ square from the second fabric.

3. Following the diagrams, appliqué the cut pieces to the base with a blind stitch. Edges that are exposed are turned under ¼″ to meet the transfer lines. Edges that have another piece appliquéd over them are stitched to the base fabric with a running stitch ⅛″ from the edge.

4. Fold under one edge at a time. Clip corners and notch angles as you go.

5. The quilt is assembled the same way as the Sweetheart Blossom Quilt, using sweat shirt fabric, flannel, or batting as filler. Quilt by hand with tiny running stitches around the edge of each appliquéd piece.

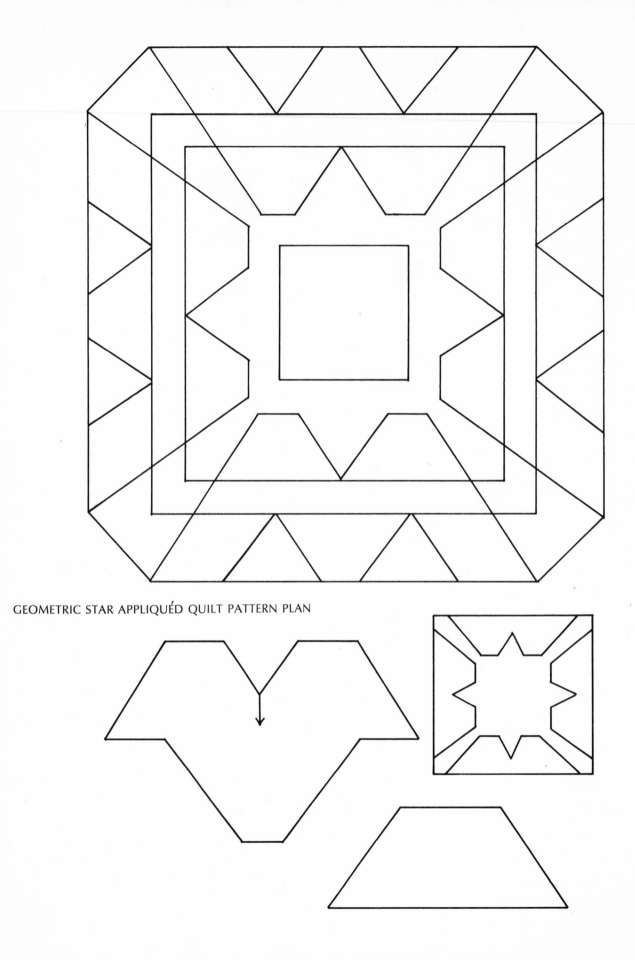

GEOMETRIC STAR APPLIQUÉD QUILT PATTERN PLAN

Pattern lines transferred onto base fabric

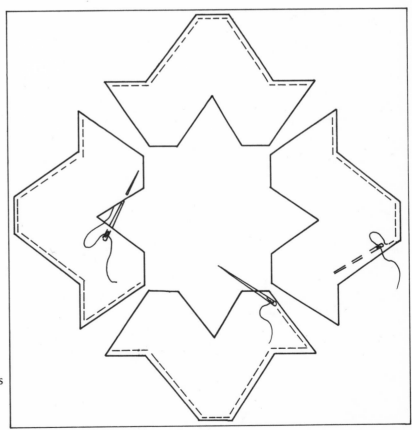

Appliqué of V-shaped pieces

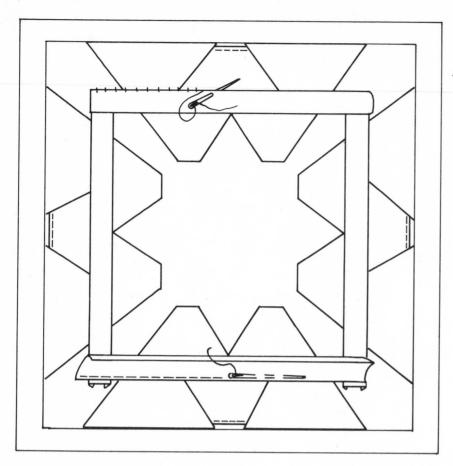

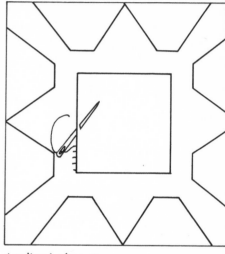

Appliqué of bands

Appliqué of center square

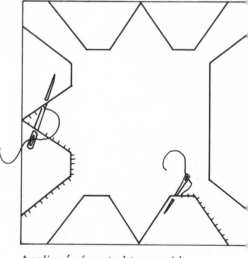

Appliqué of central trapezoids

Appliqué of center square to quilt

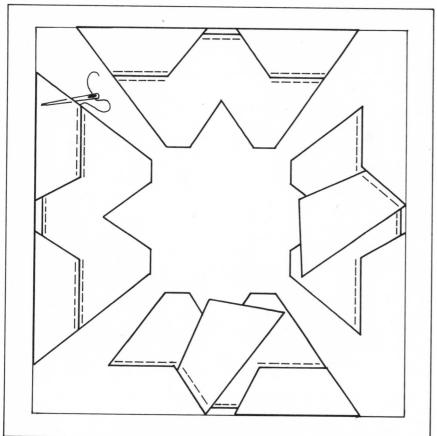

Appliqué of fabric—three trapezoids

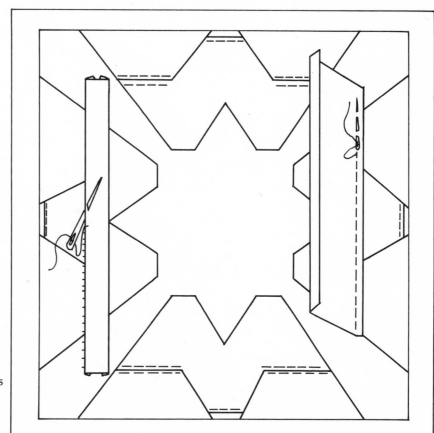

Appliqué of bands over trapezoids

Log cabin patchwork quilt by Bonnie McLean.

LOG CABIN PATCHWORK QUILT

The log cabin pattern is among the most renowned of American patchwork patterns. Books and museums everywhere exhibit quilts created in this lovely pattern.

The human-scale quilts of this pattern are composed of many squares (6″ to 12″). Each square is divided diagonally: one-half in various dark colors and one-half in various light colors. Some very lively examples are done all in light and dark printed calicos. The squares are composed of strips of fabric of the same width, sewn in overlapping boxes, radiating from a center square, usually 1″. The squares are then arranged in radiating diamond patterns, such as the one here.

Choose two lightweight woven fabrics with multiple, varicolored stripes. Look for very fine stripes—bold patterns, even if the stripes are narrow, will not work. Choose pattern colors that are different enough to create a light/dark contrast.

1. Cut thirty-six squares of the light pattern and thirty-two of the dark pattern. Using the template from the book, cut the squares on the bias. The diagonal line on the template will guide you in marking out the squares. Lay it straight on a particular stripe and cut all the squares on the stripe. This way, all of your squares (two sets) will be identical and the layout more pleasing geometrically. Cutting the squares from various center lines is also interesting.

LOG CABIN PATCHWORK QUILT PATTERN

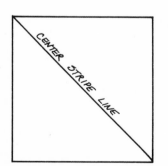

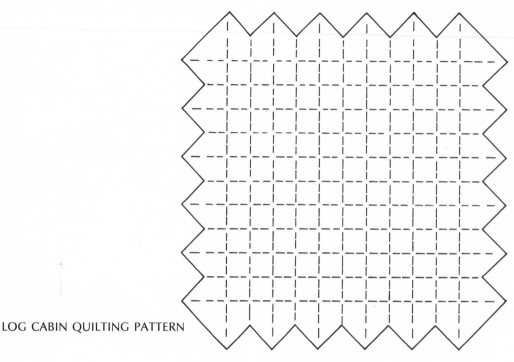

LOG CABIN QUILTING PATTERN

2. After all the squares are cut, lay them out on a large piece of flat cardboard. Arrange them in the diamond pattern, using four dark squares for the center diamond. Arrange and re-arrange the squares until you have a pattern that pleases you. There are many possible variations of arrangement. For example, you could arrange the squares to form checks or bands. The only "must" is making sure that all the stripes on a square are perpendicular to the stripes all around it.

3. Once you have established your arrangement, make a tiny mark (see pattern layout diagram) on the seam edge of each diagonal row of squares. Starting with that square, sew the cross seams of each row. Use a ¼" seam allowance and sew with a running stitch locked at each end for best results. When two squares are placed face-to-face for seaming, the stripes of both squares will run parallel. If they are perpendicular, one of the squares is not in the right position. All the seams are on the bias, so avoid easing the fabric too much in or out. Work on a table rather than on your lap.

4. After all the cross seams have been sewn, press them open. Next, stitch the lengthwise diagonal seams. In other words, sew the strips together. Match the crosswise seams, easing if necessary. Check the layout frequently. When all these seams have been sewn, press them open also. This completes the top.

5. Cut a square of lightweight fabric for the lining (approximately 10" × 10"). Lay this face down and place the batting over it. Lay the top, face up, over lining and batting and pin or baste the layers together.

Patchwork feather bed by Enid Cytrin; braided rug by Barbara Hackney; Victoriana doll by Vicky Newhouse. Photograph by Peter Schaaf.

6. Quilt by hand or machine in straight lines, working from the center lines out. Quilting lines run through the corners of each square along the diagonals.

7. The quilt is bound with single-fold bias tape. Lay the fold of the bias tape along the diagonal of the outside set of squares on two opposite sides of the quilt. Stitch with small stitches on machine or by hand. Trim the seams to ⅛". Turn the binding to the back of the quilt and blindstitch just over the seam line. Repeat binding procedure with the other two sides, folding in the ends of the binding, and blindstitch around the corners to finish.

PATCHWORK FEATHER BED

The patches are cut out on the straight grain of the fabric from narrow strips of fabric. The strips are sewn together to create stripes. The strips are then cut and staggered to create blocks.

This authentic feather bed is stuffed loosely with goose feathers. A lightly woven lightweight fabric is used for the lining to prevent the feathers from poking through.

Victorian embroidery books have a multitude of patterns to make crocheted doilies and antimacassars. They make lovely canopies. (Machine-sewn doilies work very well as a substitute; just stretch them, as in the photograph, to fit bed.)

BRAIDED RUG

Materials

Coats and Clark's Cro-Sheen mercerized cotton
    in three colors
1 roll of 2″ masking tape
Needle and thread

1. Cut crochet cotton in approximately 4′ lengths. Braid together one strand of each color into a tricolor braid. Make a solid-color braid of the darkest color. Stitch the braids together so they will not become unbraided and ravel. Braid approximately three times as much of the tricolor as of the solid color.
2. Lay out strips of the masking tape, overlapping them until you have a slightly larger surface than the size of the rug planned. Starting with the tricolor braid, lay out the braid on the sticky side. Continue round and round, alternating tricolor with solid color as desired. Be sure braids are placed very close together, but not overlapping. Also, do not allow the braid to turn over at any time.
3. As you lay the braid on the tape, you are seeing the underside of the rug. Be sure that when you come to an end that it stays on the underside of the rug, facing you. When the desired size is reached, trim the excess tape close to the rug shape.
4. Now stitch the braids together with tiny stitches, starting at the center and working round and round to the outside. Pick up only a small bit of the braid strands as you stitch to ensure that no stitches show on the right side of the rug. Trim excess frayed parts.
5. Remove the tape carefully. At this point, the rug will look cap-like and out of shape. With a steam iron, press it flat. A little spray starch applied to the underside of the rug before pressing will help to keep the rug flat and very slightly stiff.

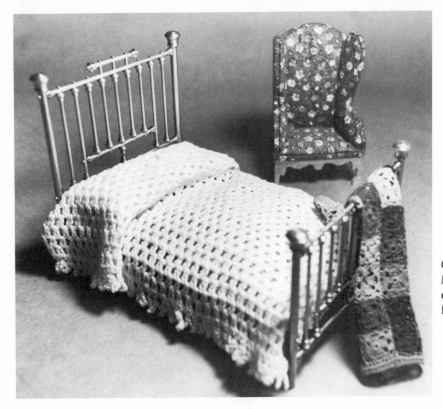

Crocheted bedspread by Rebecca Mercer-White; wing chair by Frederick Decker; granny afghan by Dottie Gulker.

CROCHETED BEDSPREAD

Ch 10, ch 1, turn.
Ch 2.
Skip 2 ch.
Make 2 dc into next chain of previous row.

The number of crocheted rows will depend on the length and width of your miniature bed. It is a nice touch to allow enough length to tuck under and drape over the pillow as they do in the finer hotels.

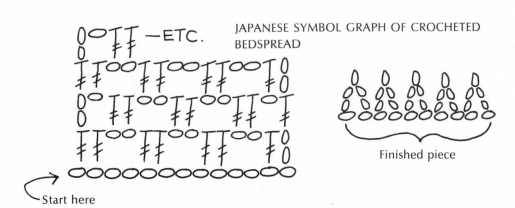

JAPANESE SYMBOL GRAPH OF CROCHETED BEDSPREAD

Start here

Finished piece

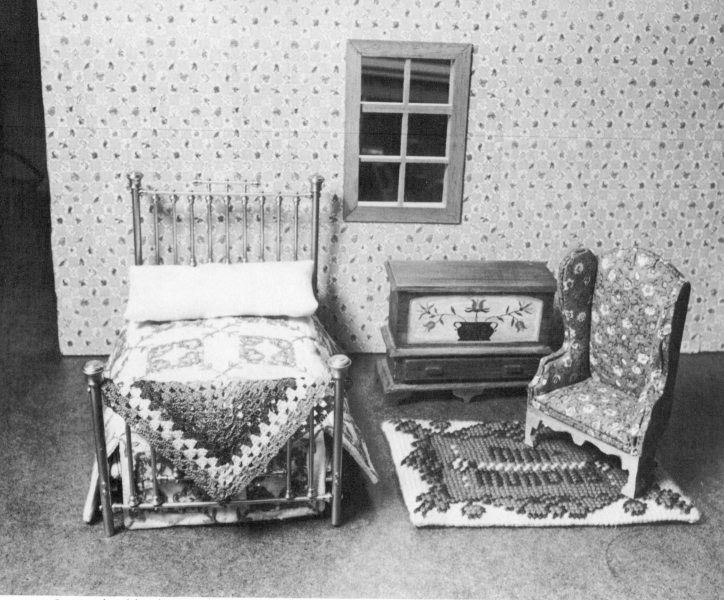

Rectangular afghan by Dottie Gulker; Mini Mundus rug by Aralee Kazdan.

CROCHETED AFGHANS

Dotty Gulker, who specializes in the finest tiny afghans, was an experienced crocheter of large afghans. Like all of the Mini Mundus crafters, she suggests that you practice on the large scale before attempting the same in miniature.

She first makes a graph to figure out the fabric and colors.

Her favorite crochet hook is a "Boye" #10. She prefers using plain sewing thread, very thin, but not polyester.

Her portable rack holds the spools, stacked on dowels for easy accessibility.

INSTRUCTIONS FOR ONE SQUARE

Using a "Boye" #10 crochet hook and very thin thread, ch 4, join
    with a slip stitch to first stitch to form a ring.
Ch 3, then 2 dc in center of ring.
Ch 1, then 3 dc; ch 1, then 3 dc; ch 1, then 3 dc.
Then ch 1 and sl st to top of first 3 ch to complete the circle.
Sl st to ch 1, then ch 3 and make 2 dc in the same ch 1.
Then ch 2 and make 3 dc in the same ch 1.
You now have one corner made.
Then ch 1 and in next ch 1, make 3 dc, then ch 2 and 3 more dc
    in the same ch 1.
You now have a second corner.
Repeat two more times and you will have one small square.

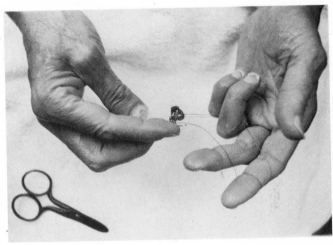

Dottie Gulker crocheting afghan.

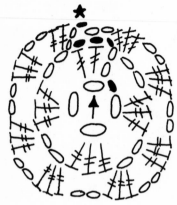

JAPANESE SYMBOL GRAPH OF CROCHETED
GRANNY AFGHAN SQUARE

Close-up of basic square.

JAPANESE SYMBOL GRAPH OF CROCHETED
SQUARE AFGHAN PATTERN

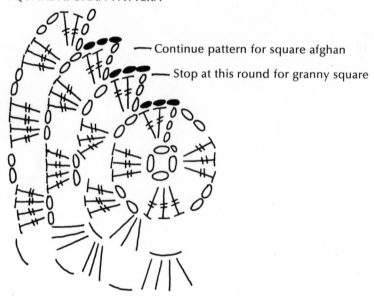

— Continue pattern for square afghan

— Stop at this round for granny square

This is the basic "granny square" that is used for square afghan, rectangular afghan (with border), and rectangular quilt, filigree.
Start at center at arrow ↑ and end at star ★.
Use granny square for pot holder, edge with slip stitch, and chain stitch a loop at one corner so pot holder can be hung.
For rectangular afghan, substitute triple crochet for double crochet and sew squares together at sides. Edge with two rows of double crochet.
For rectangular quilt, sew squares together at corners.

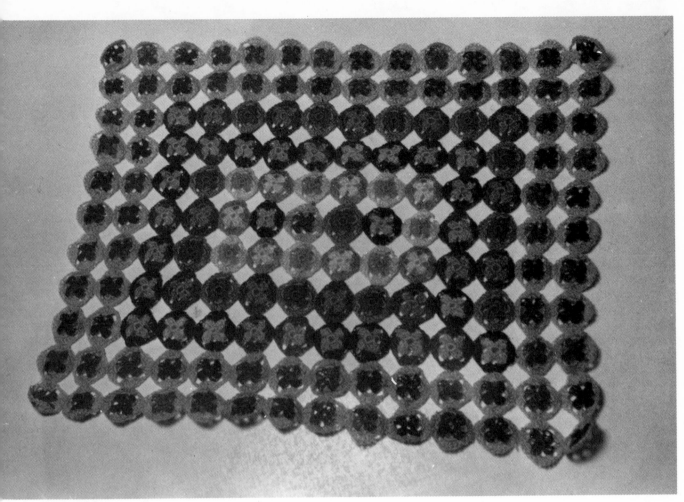

Filigree afghan.

FILIGREE AFGHAN

This is the most difficult pattern to execute. Attempt this after you have tried your hand with the other crochet patterns.

The filigree pattern has 4 squares, crocheted together, so there are no hanging threads. There are squares inside the triangles, all crocheted together.

Ch 4, join with sl st to make circle.
Ch 3 into one of the corners, sl st through the corner, ch 3, dc in circle, dc again.
Sl st into smaller of the two corners, and dc.
Repeat three more times.

Ribbon quilt by Jane Sikora.

RIBBON QUILT

Materials

2 yards each of two colors (*Green* and *White*) of
½″ ribbon
1½ yards of braid or ⅜″ lace
1 piece of white fabric, 8″ × 7½″
1 piece of fabric of a harmonizing color to be the
opposite side of the quilt, 8″ × 7½″
Embroidery thread in a color to match the
ribbon colors

1. Take a piece of white fabric 8″ × 7½″. Cut nine 8″ strips of
color *G*.
2. Lay strips on muslin, covering it completely and leaving a ⅜″
margin on the top and bottom. Baste the strips down on one
side ⅜″ from the edge.
3. Cut eleven 7¼″ strips of color *W*. Weave color-*W* strips through
color *G*. Anchor each strip with a straight pin.
4. Baste around the remaining three sides. Use braid or lace
around the edges. Insert a piece of flat, wide wire in the hem
so the quilt can be bent into the desired shape on the bed.
5. Make pillows to match—2″ by 1½″ is an appropriate size.

SILK-SCREEN QUILTS

Materials

Screen
Fabric dyes in white or colors
Extender
Turpentine
Squeegee
Calico fabric

1. Render design in black India ink on paper.
2. Photostat to size needed for quilt.
3. Give a mechanical paste-up of design to screen maker, who will frame the screen. You will have to add the hinges and base.
4. Cut the fabric pieces a little larger than the design and iron flat.
5. To print the fabric, fasten fabric on base under screen, ink on top of the screen, and pull ink over screen with squeegee. To print well, pull squeegee over screen several times.
6. To dry the material, take the piece out of the screen, lay flat, and allow to dry.

Silk-screened quilts and handkerchief bed linens by Patricia Tornborgh.

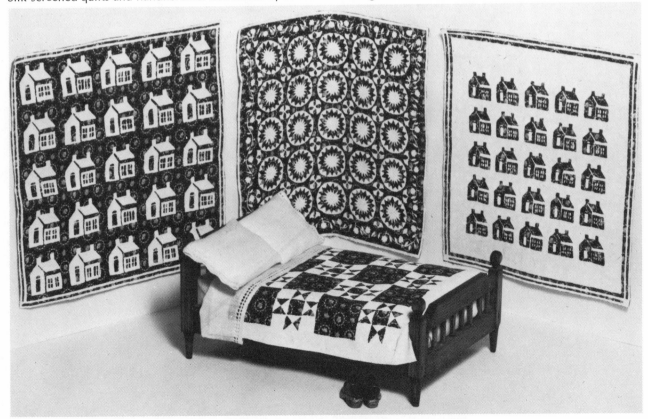

7. Fabrics used should be small-print *cotton* calicos, not synthetics, without lots of sizing in the fabric. Dark-background fabrics printed with white are the most effective.

HANDKERCHIEF LINEN SHEETS AND PILLOWCASES

Materials

2 perforated-edge linen handkerchiefs (about
$.59 each in five-and-ten)
Cotton or Kleenex for stuffing

1. Measure top dimensions of your mattress and add 2" on all sides to cover thickness and tucking. The bottom sheet is just taped to the mattress so it needs no finishing on the edges.
2. Make top sheet just long enough to fold over top, but *not* to be tucked at bottom, as too much thickness is out of scale. Hemstitch the sides of top sheet.
3. The pillows are stitched on three sides, with the decorative edge remaining the open end. Take two or three slip stitches in open end, about ¼" in from the edge, so the stuffing is not exposed.

Pillow with
lace border

78

BEDROOM KITS

Canopy bed kit by Colvin.

Realife bedroom kit.

American cross-stitch quilt and Swiss tambour curtains and scarves. A kit from Create Your Own.

Noah's Ark quilt, dust ruffle, canopy, curtains, and scarves. A kit from Create Your Own.

4
Kay Sobers's Needlepoint Specialties

PERSONAL NOTES FROM A NEEDLEPOINT EXPERT

If you ask a dozen needlepoint experts how to complete a petit point canvas, you will receive a dozen ideas. We have always been pleased with advice from Kay Sobers of Atlanta, Georgia, who has floored the miniature world's most famous collections, including Mrs. Cornelius Vanderbilt Whitney's dollhouse. On these pages we give you Kay's suggestions for copying a design, deciding on colors, yarn, and stitches, and binding or fringing your rug.

In these instructions we will assume that you have never copied a design, but that you do needlepoint. The basic stitches are described in the first chapter.

If you wish every flower, bird, dragon, etc., in a design to be perfect, then only work with graphs. The painted design when completed will look perfect and have the effect of the larger rug your design interprets. Do remember that the marker or brush will often touch a mesh and there is the tendency for one flower to have a stitch or two more than another flower in the design.

Color and harmony are very important. As you begin to plan your design, remember that you want to obtain the feel or interpretation of a large rug. A piece of miniature furniture can and should be nearly identical to the large piece from which it is copied. Rugs cannot have all the designs and details transferred to a piece of canvas measuring 6″ × 8″ or even 9″ × 12″. Therefore, we say it is an interpretation or adaptation.

Most needlepointers will be working on 18 mono canvas. This means 18 meshes to a square inch. If you are working from a graph and using 40 mesh silk gauze, naturally you can obtain more detail; however, 40 mesh silk gauze is very difficult for many of us to work on even though the results can be exquisite. For these instructions we will be using 18 mono canvas.

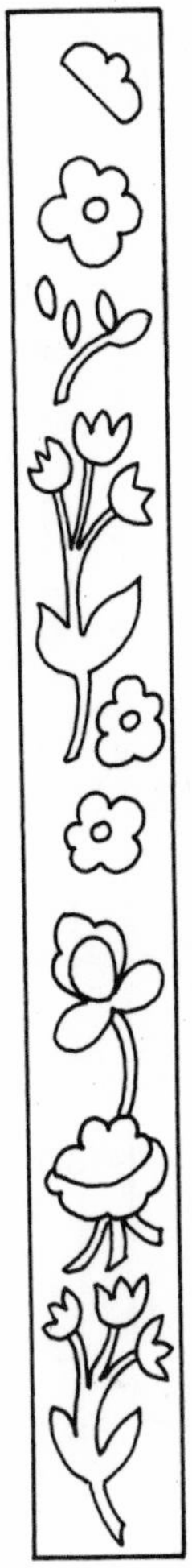

Instructions for Bell Pull

by Kay Sobers

Complete the design first and then do the background. The designs are drawn ½" to ¾" wide and 5" long. One row on either side will not distort the scale and ½" on each end is fine. The length depends entirely on the height of your ceiling. Remember if you see a little color spot on your design, use approximately four stitches and you will get the effect of a flower; one or two green stitches and you obtain the effect of a leaf. See illustration below.

Use D.M.C. Cotton Perle #5 or #8, cotton floss, crewel yarn or Persian yarn (one strand with 18 mono convas). Combine yarns to give texture to the design. Cotton Perle gives a silky look to the pull.

Finishing—After finishing the bell pull carefully roll or turn each side edge to the back and stitch or use white glue like Sobo and glue to the back of your bell pull. Trim the row canvas to ½" or less. I usually make a "V" cut in the corners and stitch or glue the ends to the back. Allow the glue to dry. If you have trouble keeping the sides down, use clothes pins to hold the canvas until it dries.

Lining—Line if possible with china silk, seam binding or some other *very thin* lining. You do not want the pull to have a bulky look. For hooks or hardware, I use jewelry findings—try looking through your old jewelry box. A hook sewn to the back makes a good hanger.

Blocking—I have never had to block a pull and that is why I have left this to the very last. Sometimes a light steam pressing adds to the finish look.

Hope you have fun making this pull.

Color spot illustration

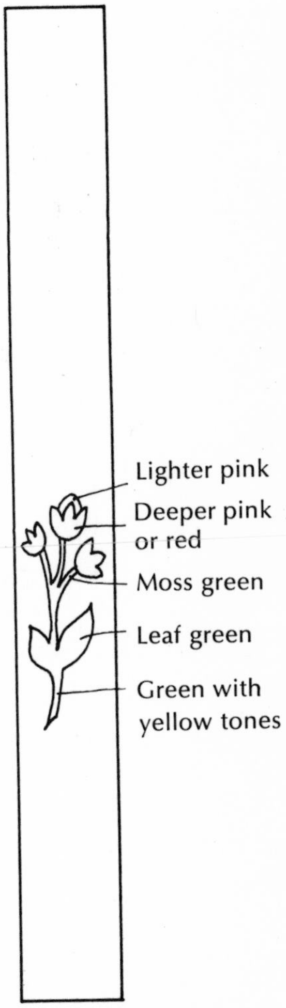

Tracing the Design

The design given for you to copy is for a rug measuring 7" × 9" and you will need a piece of white 18 mono cotton canvas that measures at least 10" × 12". This gives 1½" of unpainted border. Naturally, you can plan to have a 2" border if you feel the need for more canvas to hold in your hands or attach to your frame.

First find the center of your canvas. The easiest method is to

ROSEBUD BELL PULL

Lighter pink

Deeper pink or red

Moss green

Leaf green

Green with yellow tones

Suggestions: canvas—use 22 mono
yarn—use DMC cotton floss or perle
or use French silk floss

ORIENTAL RUG   7″ x 9″   by Kay Sobers

fold it in half and make a dot with a black Nepo marker at the fold and then fold the canvas horizontally in half and mark the center. Now count 63 meshes to the right from the center mark and mark the line, then count 63 meshes to the left of the center and mark the line. You now have the line for the 7" side of your canvas. Then count 81 meshes up from the center and mark the line; next count 81 meshes down from the center and mark the line. You now have the 9" side of your rug. With a ruler and black or gray Nepo marker or light gray Prismacolor pencil, draw your lines to make the outline for the 7" × 9" rug.

Another method is to use a ruler to mark the bottom line 7" across. Then draw one side up 9" and continue to complete the outline. Place this canvas over the design, and with very good light (some needlepointers prefer taping the design on a windowpane), begin to trace the design. Use gray or black Nepo markers or *waterproof* markers to draw the design onto the canvas. Count your borders first and draw these lines, then add the design. As you begin to draw the center medallion, be sure your canvas is in place directly over the center of the medallion. You may have to shift your canvas. Stop here for a moment. The canvas is not always perfectly straight. Do not be concerned. If your outside lines are straight, your design will be straight.

Colors

If you only plan to draw the design onto the canvas and not paint the colors onto the design, you are ready to go on to the next part.

If the artist in you wishes to get the paint and brushes out, remember to use only waterproof colors; acrylic paints, oils, AD Markers, or Flo-paque paints. Plan the colors on paper. If you are unsure of the waterproofness of your colors, then spray with an artist's matte spray to control bleeding of colors.

ORIENTAL RUG

Color and yarn suggestions:

Paternayan **Persian**

Number	Color	Where to Use	Approximate Amount
#304	Dark Blue	Outside Border	16 Strands
#385	French Blue	Outline Flowers and Scrolls	5 Strands
#386	French Blue—Medium	Scrolls in Corners	3 Strands
#395	French Blue—Lightest	Center Flowers	3 Strands
#212	Chippendale Red	Design Border and Corner Flowers, Also Center Medallion	8 Strands
#225	Rust	Color Used in Flowers Nearest to Center of Flower	3 Strands
#453	Gold	Center of Flowers and Background	20 Strands

Yarn

Take time about selecting colors. Suppose you like celadon, please select the shade you think is celadon, as there are dozens of shades of green called celadon. Light blue? Everyone has a different idea about light blue. If at all possible, go to a good needlepoint supplier and take your time about selecting colors. *You* will be living with the rug.

The types of yarn mentioned here are the ones Kay Sobers uses, but there are many others equally good. Kay likes to combine wool with silk or cotton floss. Some will say never use cotton perle. Kay uses it and finds D.M.C. cotton perle gives a lovely silk look to the rug. The shades available are extensive and luscious. Paternayan Persian and Crewel have a wide selection of colors to choose from. Do try the English Appleton Crewel yarn as well. Another possibility is a D.M.C. cotton embroidery called cotton mouline special floss, D.M.C. cotton perle #5. There is also Au Ver A Soie, a pure silk yarn from France, which is a little difficult to work with but gives a lovely sheen to the finished product. Another yarn on the market is known as Danish flower thread M. H. Matgarn, in shades of petal colors. These are a welcome addition to centers for some floral designs and as shade variations, as well as texture.

Always buy sufficient yarn and also request the color number of your yarn for future reference.

Needles

Select a good steel tapestry needle, size 20–24. Be certain it is a large enough size to thread with ease but not too large, as you do not want to stretch the mesh.

Frames

If possible, use either a frame that you sew your canvas to (top and bottom) or one that allows you to slip the canvas onto a rod and roll it up. A good idea is to tape the edges of the canvas to prevent raveling. You can paint the edges of the canvas with a decoupage coating or mod-podge to prevent raveling. It is a good idea to turn at least four meshes over and run a hem either by hand or on a sewing machine to keep the canvas from raveling. Using a frame prevents distortion and little blocking is needed when the rug is completed.

Working the Design

Kay suggests working the flowers, birds, or design first, always keeping the stitches going in the same direction. Tension is important. Do not pull yarn tightly and yet do not leave loops in the yarn. When a line is indicated, work it from the outside to the inside. If an adjustment needs to be made on the floral design, it is easier to do if the inner border line is completed before starting on the design. This is especially true for the oriental designs. Remember to work the background from side to side; this way the tension of the stitches will be the same and the background will appear even. Making an adjustment in the design is not noticeable, but the border line must be straight since the eye will see that line immediately.

Yarn Guide for 18 Mono Canvas

Persion—1 strand
Crewel—1 strand
D.M.C. Cotton Perle #5—1 strand
Appleton Crewel—2 strands

D.M.C. Cotton Mouline Special— 6 strands
French Silk Thread—3 or 4 strands
Danish Flower Thread—1 or 2 strands; use one strand for French knots

Selection of Stitch

The design may be worked in the continental stitch or the basket weave. Using a combination of stitches, and sometimes a combination of yarns, enriches the texture of the finished piece. Many crewel stitches add interest to the design.

Blocking

Blocking is usually not of major importance in the very small pieces. Steam press on the wrong side and ease the canvas into shape with your fingers. The pieces that are larger may need to be blocked. On a hard, flat surface, draw the size of the rug on white paper. Use *nonrust* tacks to tack the dampened piece (on the wrong side) and be sure you do not place the tack in the worked piece but on the raw canvas near the edge of the finished piece. Be very sure the corners are straight. Allow the piece to dry thoroughly before binding or fringing, if it is a rug you wish to fringe.

Finishing the Piece

The edges can be finished with a binding stitch. First, within ½" of the worked edge on the raw canvas, cut a small V in each corner and fold canvas back, leaving one row of canvas on each end for fringing. You can tack the sides and ends lightly to the back or use a small amount of white glue to have the edges adhere to the back. Use either seam binding, tacked carefully, or press-on tape. Remember the piece needs to have a very thin edge or appearance so as not to buckle. *Please* do not let any of your canvas show on the edges or ends. If for any reason this happens, obtain a marker close to the color of your border and touch up the white canvas. This is a must! No white edges showing!

Fringing

Use six strands of embroidery floss (mouline special). Cut strand 1½" long. With a small crochet hook, fold the canvas so one mesh is showing. Taking the crochet hook from the underside, catch loop of yarn and draw it through both pieces of mesh. Then take the two ends of the yarn and pull them through the loop. Adjust the knot with your fingers. The knot should be on the top side. As to scaling the fringe, this is slightly difficult. On most rugs the fringe length varies from less than ½" to several inches. Use your own good judgment as to the length and the size of your fringe, usually about ½" to ¾".

The depth of the pile on your rug should be as thin as possible. There is no way to determine depth. Keep the depth thin and take care that the edges are not thick with your binding stitch. Use cotton floss to bind the edges. Scale of the design appears to be more important.

There are so many excellent books on the shelves to read and study, but very few that devote space to hand-painted scaled miniature rugs. Therefore, we are still searching for answers. We would refer you to Hope Hanley's books for the binding stitch. It's easy, once you begin to work it. Do try it on a folded piece of canvas before you try it on your rug. Also, if your rug needs to be blocked, do that before doing the binding stitch and adding the fringe.

After all these instructions, we hope you have completed one rug, all the stitches going in the same direction, stitches not too tight or too loose, and finished with absolutely no white canvas showing along the four sides.

If you have youngsters in your family, start them on a design using 14 mesh, making a simple stripe rug 4" × 6". Teach them to use a needle and canvas and to create a finished piece for their own use.

FLAME STITCH SEAT COVER

This pattern is worked on 42 mesh cotton Penelope canvas and each stitch is worked over six threads of canvas. It is worked in two strands of D.M.C. floss using four colors: dark blue, crimson, orange, and pale yellow. Once the first row of the pattern has been correctly established, this is a simple pattern to work, because each row of stitching is identical to the first.

1. Cut a square of canvas 3″ × 3″, matching the straight grains of the canvas to the lines of the pattern on the graph. Fasten the pattern over the graph and trace the outline of the pattern onto the canvas with indelible ink marking the centers. Fold the canvas in corners and crease to find the center of the seat.

Petit point seat cushions by Bonnie McLean; chair from Masterpiece Miniatures.

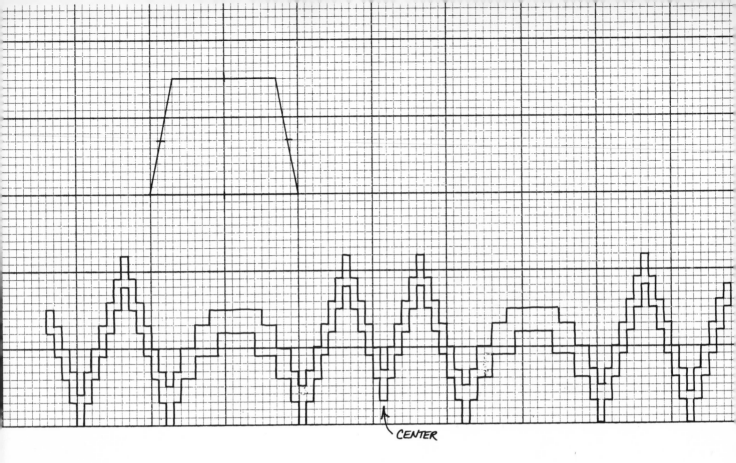

CENTER

FLAME STITCH BARGELLO SEAT COVER

2. Beginning with the yellow, work the first row of the pattern out from the center across to the outline, first one side, then the other to match. With the first row completed across to the outlines, work the next row below, from left to right, in the orange. Proceed in the next two shades, crimson and dark blue, repeating to fill into outline.

This can be done in any set of colors or monochromatically, always working from the lightest to the darkest.

FLORENTINE STITCH SEAT COVER

This pattern is based on the shading of colors. There is sufficient depth in miniature when the five colors are carefully chosen. Here we are concentrating on red and green. There are three shades of rose—medium, light, pale—and two shades of complementary green—dark and pale.

The pattern is worked on 42 mesh cotton Penelope canvas, with each stitch worked over four threads of the canvas. The design is worked in four-strand rayon floss, using two strands.

There are five colors—pale pink, rose, rose red—of the main color, and two—dark green, pale green—of the accent color.

1. Cut a 3″ × 3″ square of canvas, matching the grains of the canvas to the lines on the pattern on the graph. Trace outline onto canvas with indelible ink, marking top and bottom center.
2. Working from the center, stitch first row of pale pink (main line on graph), working to, but not past, the outline. Next, work pale green, then dark green, red, rose, and pale pink again.
3. Working from the center of the top outline, work pale pink down from the peak of first line of pattern. Work first line of pattern across to outline, then work, with pale pink, the other side of the first line.
4. Work in the medium rose, as shown on graph, under the peaks of the pale pink. Then work the rose red, dark green, and pale green to complete first run of pattern. Then go back to pale pink and repeat first line.

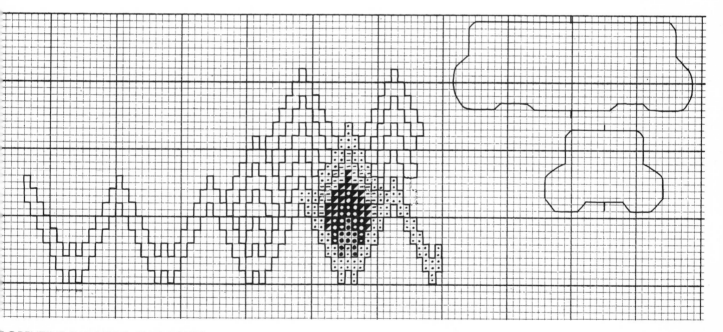

FLORENTINE BARGELLO SEAT COVER

HUNGARIAN POINT FLORAL STAIR RUNNER

This pattern is worked in three strands of D.M.C. floss on 36 mesh cotton Penelope canvas. The stitches are worked vertically between every pair of threads of the canvas and horizontally over every four threads. Four squares of the graph represent one stitch.

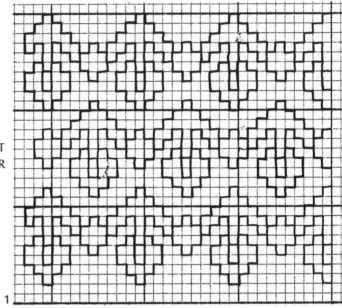

HUNGARIAN POINT
FLORAL STAIR RUNNER

The runner could also be worked horizontally over two threads, giving a shorter pattern (see graph 2) but it will take twice as long to finish.

Runner shown is 3″ wide for 4″-wide staircase. Background is medium blue with dark blue diamonds. The flowers are maroon and dusty pink with bright green stems and leaves.

1. Cut a strip of canvas 5″ wide from selvage to selvage. Measure your stair step across, deciding how wide you want your runner to be. Add the width of step to the height of the riser and multiply by the number of steps to determine the length.
2. Starting at the bottom line count up ten threads and mark a line across: repeat three or four times more. Starting from the bottom left corner, divide the vertical threads the same way. This will give a guide for the first few rows of work.
3. This pattern is worked in rows of stitches across the width of the runner. There are seven rows of stitches to each repeat of the pattern. Starting from the bottom left-hand corner, work the first row of stems and leaves, matching the guidelines on

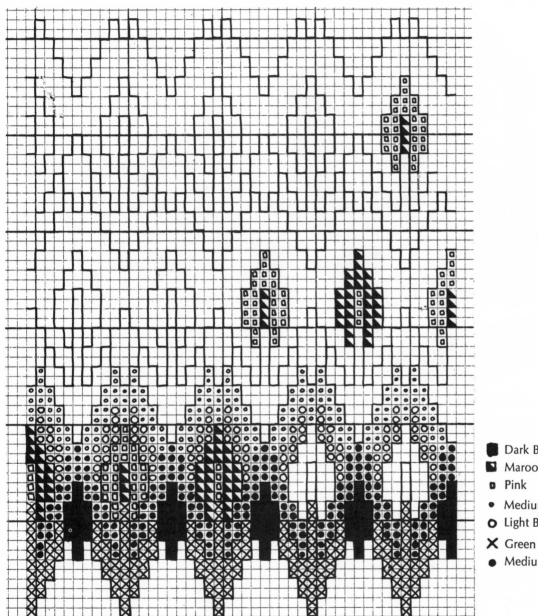

	Dark Blue
	Maroon
	Pink
	Medium Blue
	Light Blue
	Green
	Medium Dark Blue

HUNGARIAN POINT FLORAL STAIR RUNNER

2

Hungarian point floral stair runner.

the canvas to the heavy lines on the graph. Next work row two in background blue. Row three is the dark blue. Work rows four and five in background color.

4. Then work the next row in green. After working a few repeats of the pattern, work in the alternating flowers. The flowers can be worked in diagonal rows up the runner rather than across. This makes the diagonal color repeat less confusing.

5. Coloring the graph will make things much easier getting started. This pattern can be worked in any set of five colors. If you would like all the flowers to be the same color, you will need an accent color for the centers.

6. If the length of the staircase is greater than the width of the canvas, make two pieces and fit to inside angle of riser, matching the pattern for the beginning of the second piece.

7. When you approach the end of the piece, fit it to the staircase. The thickness of the needlework may change the length of the runner, making it too short.

EMBROIDERED COAT OF ARMS FOR
FIRE SCREEN

This piece is worked in D.M.C. floss, soie de perse, or silk buttonhole thread. The stitches used are the satin stitch, straight stitch, outline stitch, and couching stitch, in silk, gold, and silver threads on satin or fine damask brocade background.

EMBROIDERED FIRE SCREEN

Embroidered coat of arms fire screen by Bonnie McLean; wood stand and frame by Donald Dube.

1. Cut a square of steel blue satin big enough to fit over your embroidery hoop. Cut a piece of cotton batiste or similar cloth the same size as the satin. Lay the satin under the page with the design on it, making sure the grain of the fabric runs straight through the design. Put a piece of carbon paper between the satin and the page and transfer the design to the satin, using a sharp pencil. Because of the intricacy of the design, it is necessary to use the sharpest pencil possible.

2. Lay the satin over the batiste, straight grain to straight grain, and put them both into your hoop. Start and end all stitches in batiste. First work the couching. Couch six strands of gold embroidery floss, or one of the metallic yarns with one strand of silk. Use a large needle to bring the metallic thread through the cloth. Use a dark color (peacock blue) in the lower left and upper right corners of the shield. Use a light color (yellow) in the upper left and lower right corners. For couching the gold, it is not as important that you follow the lines exactly as it is that you make both sides the same. Work out from the center line on one part and then match the corresponding part.

3. Next work the larger inner areas. Work the chevron in pale salmon, starting from the center line out to the couched line and keeping the stitches straight on the grain of the satin.

4. Next, in white, work the center portion above the chevron in a satin stitch, then in yellow work a satin stitch to either side of the white. Carefully work the fleur de lis, in a satin stitch with a silver metallic thread (using three strands of six-strand metallic embroidery thread), with a crewel needle big enough to take the thread. Match the stitches from side to side. Then work an outline stitch around the fleur de lis in a darker salmon pink.

5. Work the swords in a straight stitch in peacock blue, over the white. Work the emblems in the corners in a straight stitch, using blue, white, and salmon.

6. Center fire-screen frame over design, stretching out bubbles between satin and batiste. Mark the inside corners lightly with a pencil. Run a basting stitch around the design ¼" from the marks and remove from the hoop.

HUNGARIAN POINT FLORAL CARPET

This pattern is designed for 20 mesh single canvas. Each stitch is worked over two threads of canvas. On 20 mesh, using graph as one-quarter of the finished rug, the rug will be approximately 8″ × 10″. The rug can be larger or smaller by adding or subtracting repeats. A full repeat will add 1″ in length and slightly more than 1″ in width.

o Red

■ Pink

◨ Aqua

✕ Blue

● Background

HUNGARIAN POINT FLORAL PRINT CARPET

Hungarian point floral carpet.

A finer canvas can be used for a more petite stitch and pattern. This will also decrease the size of the rug unless repeats are added. A 20 mesh Penelope canvas used singly will produce a rug 4″ × 5″ unless repeats are added. A canvas any larger than 20 would be too large for miniature effect, but any size smaller is all right.

1. To determine finished size on chosen canvas, divide mesh size by 160 for the width and by 200 for the length. Each additional repeat will add 20 meshes to the length and 22 to the width.
2. This pattern requires five pattern colors and a background color. Color in the five pattern colors on the graph for easy reference. On 20 mesh you can use two strands of Persian wool. On finer mesh, use either the very fine petit point wools (Appleton or Medici) or D.M.C. cotton.

3. Work a sample 1″ square on a scrap of canvas to determine how many strands you need of whatever yarn you decide to use. Try a couple of samples with different numbers of strands and different needles.

4. When you have established your yarn and needle choice, fold the canvas (cut 4″ larger than finished rug size—length and width) into quarters and crease to find the center. With sharp pencil, divide between the center threads, crosswise and lengthwise. Working from the center, divide into groups of eleven threads lengthwise and groups of ten crosswise. These are guidelines that will help show you where to repeat the pattern.

5. Matching the pattern from bottom left, start in the center of the canvas by working the geometric diamonds. Count *very* carefully, as these areas will make an easy reference for other parts of the pattern. Work each of the flowers and diamonds separately, ending the threads rather than running them across the back of the canvas. After the diamonds, work the stems of the flowers and then the two flower colors. Next work the secondary accent color and then the background. On the background, work in rows across the canvas from border to border.

6. If you add an uneven number of repeats (i.e., 1 or 3), remember to reverse the direction of the flowers to keep the pattern continuous.

VICTORIAN PETIT POINT CARPET

This carpet, which is 6″ × 8″ or 6″ × 7″, is surprisingly less complex than it looks, but it is not recommended for those not experienced in working curves in petit point.

1. Choose a canvas from 24 to 48 mesh and six or seven colors of applicable type of yarn. Cut your canvas to 10″ × 12″.

2. Fasten the canvas over the pattern, making sure that the lines of the canvas match the straight outside lines of the pattern. Use big paper clips or large bobby pins to hold the canvas firmly to the page. Using indelible ink, trace the outlines of the design onto the canvas.

3. After preparing the canvas, color the picture, using the colors you want for your decor. Start with three or four main colors that you wish to use, adding, at most, three accent colors as you choose, or you can transfer the design to another piece of paper and color it there if you do not wish to color in your book. Divide the drawing into quarters and color one-quarter at a time. You might want to change some colors as you see the

VICTORIAN PETIT POINT RUG

design fill in. When you think you have what you want, try the color draft on the floor of the room, not for actual color but for color arrangement.

When you are satisfied with the design, you are ready to work it. On this scale, it is better not to paint in the colors on the canvas. Use your color draft as a reference as you go. Test your yarn and needle on a corner of the canvas for coverage and texture.

4. Use a small hoop on the canvas and work with one hand under and one hand above, passing the needle back and forth through the canvas. Work as much in basket-weave stitch as possible. It is recommended that you work the larger flat areas first to stabilize the canvas around the more complex areas.

5. The design as transferred to the canvas will not be totally symmetrical. If you like working counted threads, transfer only one-quarter of the design onto the canvas. Work that quarter and then match the remaining quarters to the first.

6. The rug size can be reduced by eliminating the sections shown on the pattern.

CHINESE CARPET—HAPPINESS PATTERN

The rug is 10″ × 6½″. It is worked on 22 mesh canvas in two strands of wool.

1. The pattern given in the book is one-quarter of the pattern of the full rug. This piece can be done most easily with counted threads because of its intricacy. If you don't desire to work counted threads, the pattern can be transferred to a graph paper the same size as the mesh on your canvas; then transfer it to your canvas, making sure that the lines on the graph run parallel to the grain of the canvas. It is done in two shades of each of three complementary colors.

2. Work the main outlines in a basket-weave stitch, fill in the motif with a continental stitch. Last, work the background in a basket-weave stitch.

3. Block and bind off, using narrow satin ribbon as the rug binding.

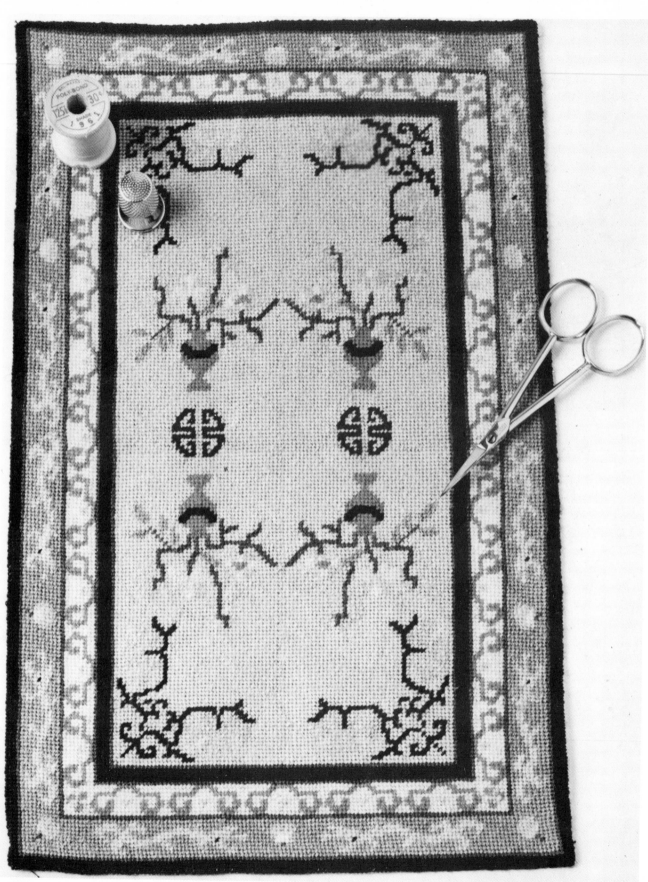

Chinese carpet by anonymous craftsman.

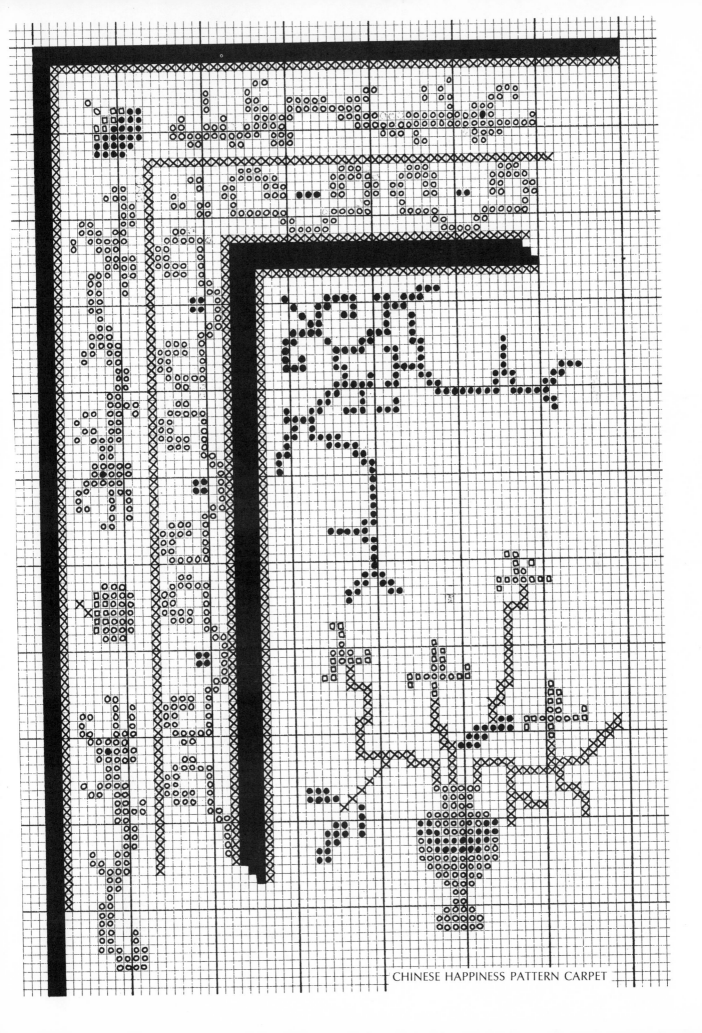

CHINESE HAPPINESS PATTERN CARPET

ORIENTAL RUG—GOOD LUCK PATTERN

This pattern is easier to count out than to transfer to the canvas. The pattern is very symmetrical and would be difficult to transfer symmetrically.

The carpet measures 3¾" × 5½", not including the ½" fringe on 24 mesh canvas. It is worked in navy blue, Chinese red, and white. The size of the rug can be varied by changing the size of the canvas and yarn or by adding repeats of the pattern. The yarn used is extra fine petit point wool or one strand of Persian yarn.

ORIENTAL GOOD LUCK PATTERN CARPET

1. First work the navy blue in a continental stitch. Do the inside border first, next work the octagons and good luck signs, and finally the outside borders. Next work the red and then the white, all in a basket-weave stitch.
2. Block the work. After blocking, bind the rug, leaving one row of thread exposed to attach the fringe. The fringe is 1½" pieces of off-white petit point wool, individually looped through each space in the canvas with a tiny crochet hook.
3. This rug has a lining of sateen stitched to the back along the edge of the stitching and fringe.

The table pictured in the photograph is made of velvet and lace.

Oriental rug by Bonnie McLean; Tiffany lamp by Robert von Fliss; bust of Mozart, vase, and velvet skirted table from Mini Mundus shop.

PETIT POINT SEAT COVER

PETIT POINT SEAT COVER

This 1½″ × 1¼″ piece is worked on 42 mesh silk canvas. It is worked in three colors of green, three of pink, and two of blue, using two strands of six-strand D.M.C. cotton.

1. This project must be worked on a hoop. So get a tiny hoop and cut the canvas just big enough to fit it.
2. Lay canvas over design in the book and transfer with indelible pen. Hoop canvas and work design using basket-weave stitch wherever possible. Work the background in a basket-weave stitch.
3. Remove from hoop, block, and mount on your chair seat.

Petit point chair cushion by Bonnie McLean; needlepoint cushions by Helene Kreda; window from Houseworks; chair and sofa from Americana Miniatures; window shade by Artie Marcus; brass cups from Clare-Bell Brassworks.

DIAGONAL NEEDLEPOINT PILLOW

This pillow design, using a three-color combination, is useful for "pulling together" the color scheme of a room setting. It helps to accent colors in wallpaper and upholstery. Use thin velvet or felt for the backing. This particular pattern is worked according to dark, medium, and white colors. Attractive combinations can be achieved using brown, beige, and white; or red, pink, and white; or green, turquoise, and white, etc.

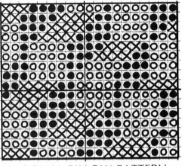

DIAGONAL PILLOW PATTERN

HOME SWEET HOME NEEDLEPOINT PILLOW

Every dollhouse needs a Home Sweet Home pillow. The pattern can be worked in any four contrasting colors, starting first with the letters, leaving the background for last.

HOME SWEET HOME PILLOW
Use needlepoint cross stitch.
Do letters first, then background.
This pattern can be done in any two contrasting colors.

WHISTLER'S MOTHER NEEDLEPOINT PILLOW

This is one of the most popular pillows at Mini Mundus. The combination of silver, gray, black, and white achieves a stunning resemblance to the famous painting, in miniature.

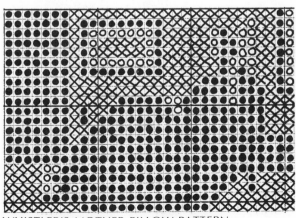

WHISTLER'S MOTHER PILLOW PATTERN

Whistler's Mother pillow in needlepoint by Irma Cohen.

BUTTERFLY PILLOW

This delightful little pillow takes no time to make and blends into any decorative scheme. A bright-colored backing adds a charming touch.

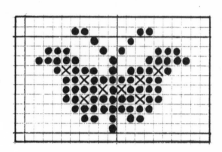

Butterfly pillow in petit point
by Bonnie McLean.

NEEDLEPOINT KITS

There are now specially designed needlepoint kits for miniature enthusiasts. The photographs presented here give you a general idea of the kits available on the market. At the back of the book, in the Appendix, you will also find the names of professionals who will create original designs for you, as well as supply needlepoint kits. Generally, the kits are for 18 mono canvas, but if you are ordering a special design, you can certainly specify mesh size.

Remember, *don't ruin your eyes;* work with a magnifying glass. We have had several reports at Mini Mundus of women who have damaged their eyesight by working too many long hours without using a magnifying glass.

Blue Persian petit point rug, 5½″ x 7½″. A kit from Create Your Own.

Red oriental petit point rug, 8″ x 10″. Design printed in full color. A kit from Create Your Own.

Colonial eagle petit point rug, 8″ x 10″, octagon shape. A kit from Create Your Own.

Fringed floral oval living room rug, pillows, picture, footstool cover. A kit from Create Your Own.

Dining room petit point rug with four chair covers and bell pull. A kit from Create Your Own.

Child's alphabet petit point nursery rug, 5″ x 7″, pictures and pillows. A kit from Create Your Own.

Green Aubusson petit point rug, 8″ x 11″. A kit from Create Your Own.

Blue Chinese Ming petit point rug, 8" x 10". A kit from Create Your Own.

Red Bokhara scatter rug, 4½" x 4½". A kit from Create Your Own.

Red Bokhara petit point rug, 6½" x 6½". A kit from Create Your Own.

Blue Kerman octagon petit point rug, 4" x 4". A kit from Create Your Own.

Chinese dragon petit point rug, 4½" x 4½". A kit from Create Your Own.

Hand-painted canvas. A kit from Vicki Fox.

Pink or blue rose garland petit point rug, 8" x 11". A kit from Create Your Own.

5
Window Treatments

Look in the handkerchief and lace department of shops and thrift
bazaars. Handkerchiefs and laces are easily converted into curtains, as well as into bed linens, towels, and shower curtains.

Usually each curtain is the width of the window. Draperies
are slightly longer than the window or down to the floor. And for
a regal touch, draperies can spill over slightly upon the floor.

Spraying curtains with unscented hair spray helps to keep the
fabric in place.

There are various ways to hang a curtain.

1. Insert screw eyes into the window frame to support a
   brass rod or dowel.
2. Hammer straight pins through the tops of curtains and
   into the wall.
3. Place dabs of Mini Hold along the tops of curtains and also
   to attach sides to wall. Press to hold.
4. Use small thumbtacks to hold up brass rod or dowel.

You can also utilize iron-on webbing when making curtains.
Pleats can be formed by fusing narrow strips of fusible web
(Stitch Witchery) with an iron set at medium heat. Trim can also
be pressed into place using the fusible web.

TIEBACK CURTAINS AND BEDSPREAD

Fabrics

Lightweight soft fabrics are the easiest to handle. Use light cottons, silks, linens, or synthetics. Beware of stiff fabrics! They will not gather or drape.

Prints must be small. Use tiny floral patterns, stripes, or geometrics. In fact, use whatever appeals to you, but remember, the scale in most dollhouses is 1" to 1'!

Trim

Use tiny lace, eyelet, ribbon, fringe, braid, or any appropriate edging. Just think small! Sewing can be done by machine or by hand. Glue (Sobo) is also a convenient aid to dollhouse decorating.

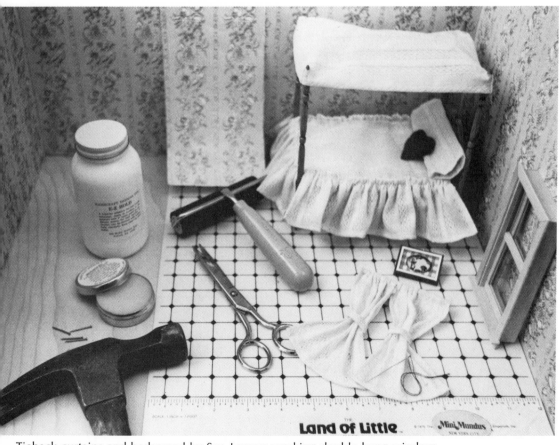

Tieback curtains and bedspread by Sue Lerner; working double-hung window from Houseworks; miniature papier-maché picture from P. J.'s Miniature Reflections; E-Z hold wallpaper paste, 1" to 1' ruler and Mini Hold wax from Mini Mundus lumberyard.

Tieback Curtains

1. Measure the width of the window frame. Add ½".
2. Measure the length from the rod to the floor, sill, or apron. Add ½".
3. Make a paper pattern using these measurements.
4. Pin paper on fabric. Cut.
5. On side edges, turn under ¼". Press. Turn under another ¼" and stitch. On lower edge, turn ¼". Press. Turn under another ¼" and stitch. (This is the way "real" patterns read; you might cheat the way we do and do it all at once!) On top edge, turn

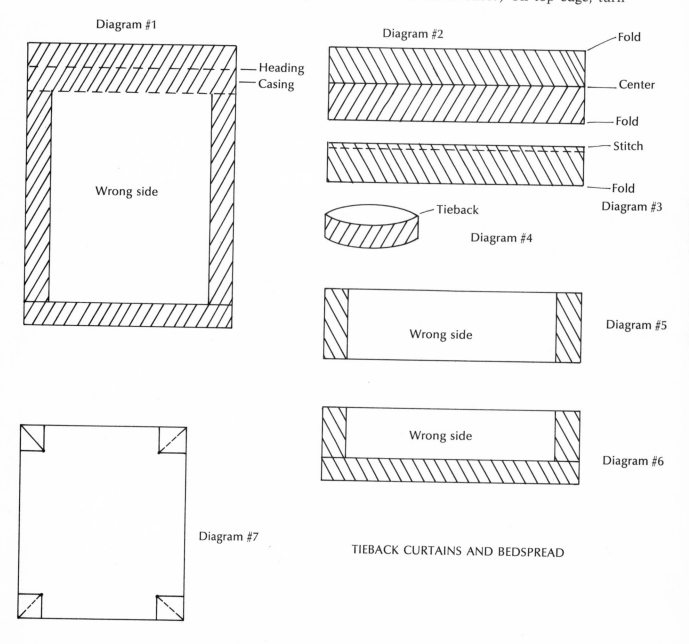

TIEBACK CURTAINS AND BEDSPREAD

116

under ¼". Make two seams for casing and heading (diagram 1).

6. For the tiebacks, cut two strips of fabric 2½" long and 1" wide. Fold in ¼" on raw edges (diagram 2).

7. Fold on center line and stitch (diagram 3).

8. Sew ends together to form the tieback (diagram 4).

Bedspread

1. Measure the length of the bed. Add 1".
2. Measure the width of the bed. Add 1".
3. Make a paper pattern. Pin pattern on fabric and cut. Turn under ¼" on all edges. Press. Turn under another ¼" and stitch.
4. For ruffles, measure the distance from the bed to the floor. Add 1¼".
5. Double the measurement of the length of the bed and add 1".
6. Double the measurement of the width of the bed. Add 1".
7. Make a paper pattern for side and end ruffles. Pin patterns to fabric.
8. Cut two side ruffles and one end ruffle.
9. Turn under ¼" on all side edges. Press. Turn under another ¼" and stitch (diagram 5).
10. Turn under ¼" on all bottom edges. Press. Turn under another ¼" and stitch (diagram 6).
11. For gathers, turn under ¼" at top of ruffles. Using a long basting stitch, sew ¼" from top. Pull gathers to fit bedspread.
12. Pin ruffles to bedspread. Sew ruffles to the bedspread.
13. For canopy, measure the distance between the bedposts. Add 2" to the width and 2" to the length.
14. Make paper pattern. Mark holes for bedposts on pattern. Pin pattern on fabric and cut.
15. Make holes for bedposts (we use a closed scissors!).
16. If you're very energetic, finish by using a buttonhole stitch in the post holes (diagram 7).
17. To miter corners, fold on center broken line (right sides together). Bring solid lines together and stitch. Turn excess toward end. Turn under ¼" on all edges. Press. Turn under another ¼" and hem by hand.

Pillow

The average pillow is 1¼" × 2¼".

1. Using the scale 1" to 1', make a paper pattern for pillow, allowing ¼" for all seams.
2. Cut two pieces of fabric. Put right sides together. Sew around three edges. Turn.

3. Stuff with cotton. Sew open end by hand.
4. For pillow sham, make a paper pattern 2″ × desired length plus 1″. Pin pattern to fabric on the fold and cut.
5. Open fabric. Turn under ¼″ on raw edges. Press.
6. Turn under another ¼″. Stitch.
7. Fold fabric right sides together. Sew remaining open edge. Turn.
8. If you're ambitious, add ruffles! Voilá.

Finis. Have fun!

CUSTOM-MADE CURTAINS

Mrs. Kathe LaTour enjoys creating custom-made curtains. Her favorite materials are batiste cotton, old lace, and rickrack. If there is no view outside her window, she cuts out a scene from a photograph and glues it behind the frame.

Tieback curtain with lace by Kathe LaTour.

CURTAINS, BRODERIE ANGLAISE
(LACE AND EMBROIDERY)

These curtains are made from white cotton floss on white organza, using the buttonhole, running, and double back stitches.

1. Use a short, fine quilting needle for stitching and a pointed awl or punch to open the holes.
2. Fasten the organza over the pattern, matching the straight grains of the fabric to the straight lines in the book. Trace the pattern onto the organza with a fine sharp pencil.
3. It is strongly recommended that you get an oval loop that will fit the whole curtain surface (approximately 9″). Lace is very delicate and stretching a worked portion over the edge of the hoop could damage it. Lay out a square of white felt over the hoop and cut it out ½″ from the edge of the hoop. Rehoop with organza over felt, making sure that the threads of the organza run straight and perpendicular and the organza is taut.

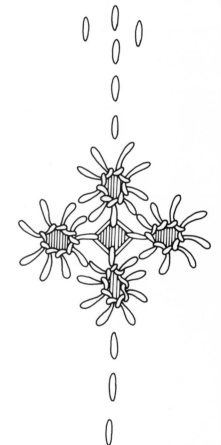

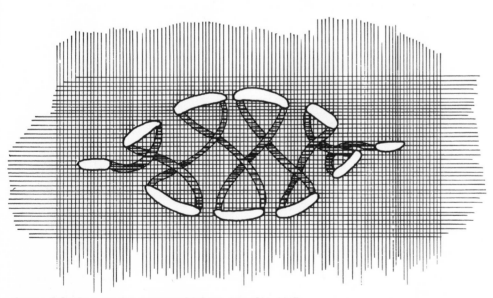

OPEN DOUBLE BACK HERRINGBONE STITCH AND
EYELET STITCH FOR CURTAINS

BRODERIE ANGLAISE
CURTAINS PATTERN

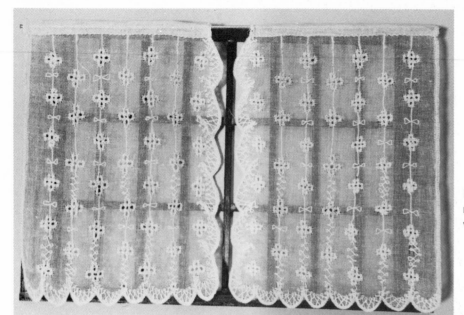

Broderie anglaise curtains by Bonnie McLean; twenty-four panel window from Houseworks.

Close-up of broderie anglaise in progress.

4. When beginning the stitching, run end of thread along line, backwards of starting point. Weave the thread into the fabric; this takes only a few stitches and you eliminate a knot; then work the embroidery over it. Work a fine running stitch along the outside scallop line. Work a double backstitch (herringbone) on back from inside scallop line to the running stitch. This is called shadow work. To trace the shadow work lines, lay pieces face down on white paper and go over inside scallop lines with sharp pencil.

5. Next, work fine, close buttonhole stitch over running stitch on edge of scallops.

6. To make the eyelets, starting at top center make a running stitch down dotted line to first diamond of dots. With the thread on the back of the work, put the punch through the top dot, spreading the threads as much as possible without breaking them. This makes a hole about $\frac{3}{16}''$ in diameter. Bring the needle through the hole and work the first buttonhole stitch from the center of the diamond to the hole. Make eight more buttonhole stitches around the hole. Make the stitches through the bias, the only stitch that runs through the straight grain is in the center of the diamond. Stitches made straight to the grain draw the threads of cloth together, making holes where you don't want them. On the last buttonhole stitch, put the needle through the loop of first and drop the needle back. Punch the next hole to the right or left of first and repeat the process around to the first buttonhole stitch in that hole. Do this for all four dots in the diamond. Run the thread through the back of the bottom eyelet and make a running stitch to the next set of eyelets.

7. Work double backstitch instead of running stitch in oval areas.

8. A cross on the diagram indicates a shadow. Work X on the back. End the threads under the eyelets weaving them under the stitches. Start threads in this manner also.

9. Because of the fragility of the material, if you make an error, it is better to leave it and change the design to accommodate the error.

10. After the embroidery is done, wash if necessary, handling delicately to avoid crinkling. Block curtain on clean white paper, pinning well beyond edges of fabric. When dry, fold long edge along line to back of curtain and work fine, close, even buttonhole stitch over fold. Cut excess material away from back close to buttonhole edging. Carefully cut material away around scallops, being very careful not to cut the stitches.

11. Make a tiny folded hem at the top of the curtain.
12. To make matching curtain, transfer the design in the same manner as you did for the first curtain. Lay the fabric face down on a piece of white paper and go over the lines. This side now becomes the face.

CROCHETED CURTAINS

These curtains are easiest for beginners. They take approximately one hour each at first. They also look fancier than they really are. The curtains utilize the basic chain stitch (ch). Window size is 2″ × 2″.

Materials

Size 3 hook
Mercerized crochet or bedspread cotton

Ch 23, turn.
Hdc in 2nd ch from lp.
Hd in each of remaining chains.
Ch 1, turn.
One more row of hdc.
Ch 2 and turn.
Dc in 1st hdc from lp.
Ch 2.
Skip 2 hdc.
1 dc each in next 2 hdc.
Continue pattern to end of row.
Ch 5 and turn.
Skip 5 ch and sc in 5th sc. Repeat three more times.
Ch 3 and dc in last sc of previous row.
Ch 5, turn.
Sc in middle of chain 5 lp. Repeat three more times.
Ch 3 and dc first sc of previous row.
Continue until desired length is reached.
Edge or Border: 1 sc in each of 4 dc.
Ch 3.
Sc in next dc.
Sc in each of next 3 dc.
Ch 3.
Sc in next dc.
Continue pattern.

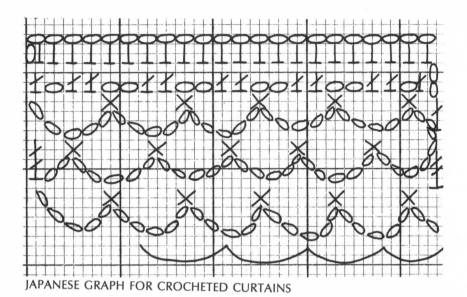

JAPANESE GRAPH FOR CROCHETED CURTAINS

Crocheted curtains and tablecloth by Rebecca Mercer-White.

TABLECLOTH

Ch 4; join with sl st to form circle.

1st Rnd: ch 2; 6 dc in ring; join in 2nd ch of ch 2.

2nd Rnd: ch 2; 2 dc in each dc; join in same manner.

3rd Rnd: ch 2; 2 dc in each dc; join.

4th Rnd: ch 2; 1 dc in first dc; 2 dc in next dc; continue, increase 1 dc in every 2nd dc; join.

5th Rnd: ch 2; 1 dc in first dc; 1 dc in next dc; 2 dc in next dc; continue increasing 1 dc in every 3rd dc.

6th Rnd: ch 2; increase 1 dc in every 4th dc; continue pattern.

Continue until diameter of circle equals diameter of tabletop.

Continue 1 dc in each dc without increasing until tablecloth is ½″ from floor.

Divide total number of stitches by 12. That number becomes your increase number (e.g., if the increase number is 9, continue 1 dc in each dc for 8 stitches. 2 dc in 9th dc; continue pattern).

Edge or Border: 1 sc in each of 4 dc; ch 3; sc in next dc; sc in each of next 3 dc; ch 3; sc in next dc; continue pattern.

VELVET DRAPES

Mrs. Kathe LaTour cuts out red velvet for her version of drapes and a valance (minus the valance box). The trim is of gold braid and the lace curtain is from the hem of an antique "pettiskirt."

The window is 4″ × 8″; the panel is 3″ × 9″.

Materials

1 piece of fabric, 6½″ × 10″

1 piece of lace, 4″ × 9″

1. Cut the fabric in half so that you have two pieces, each 3¼″ × 10″.
2. Sew a ¼″ hem in the long sides and a ½″ hem in the short sides.
3. Cut out a piece of lace 4″ × 9″ and sew a ½″ hem on the 4″ sides.
4. Place the lace curtain between the pair of drapes on a thin brass rod.
5. Pull the drapes down taut and tack them into place with tiny nails. Allow the curtains to hang free.

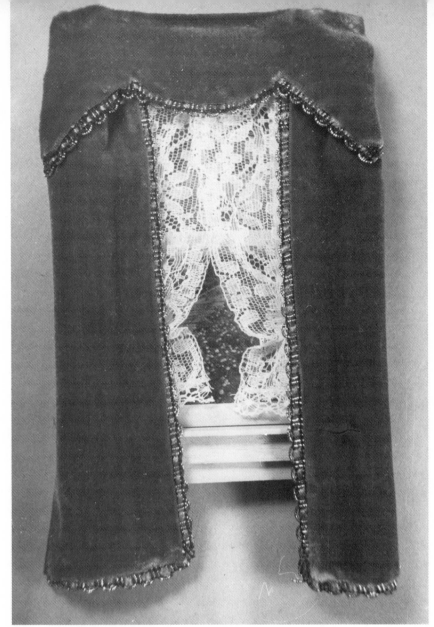

Velvet draperies by Kathe LaTour.

VALANCE BOX

Materials

1 strip of basswood, ⅛" × 1"
Razor saw
White glue
1 piece of the fabric used for the drapes, 7" × 2"
1 piece of trim, 8", for festoons if desired

1. Cut out and assemble the pieces of basswood as shown in the
   plans.

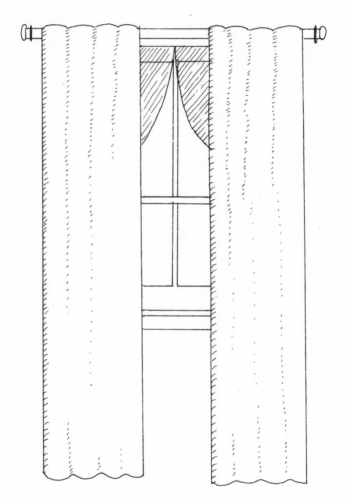

Top View

DRAPES AND VALANCE

2. Cover with the piece of drapery fabric.
3. Add the festoons if desired, draping them as shown in the sketch.
4. Glue valance box to wall over window.

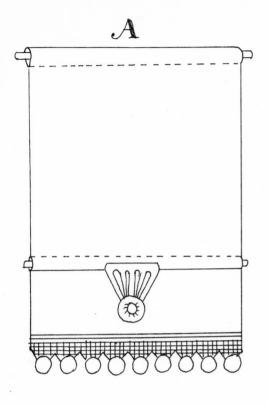

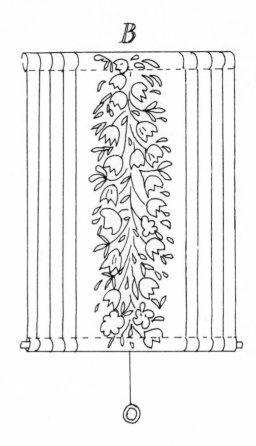

WINDOW SHADES
Actual size

WINDOW SHADES AND HARDWARE

Cottons make the best fabric for miniature window shades. A $\frac{1}{16}''$ dowel, cut slightly longer than the width of the window-pane, will extend properly at the top of the window frame. Another dowel can be placed near or at the bottom of the shade.

Shackman produces an expandable brass curtain rod for $1. Tiny decorative balls are at each end of the rod. Use screw eyes or bent pins to hold up the ends of the dowels.

Plain brass tubing can easily be cut to the desired length for pennies. But there is a problem to finding loose brass balls that can be affixed at each end.

Colonial Craftsman offers pewter tiebacks to decorate your window treatment. They can be painted to match your decor.

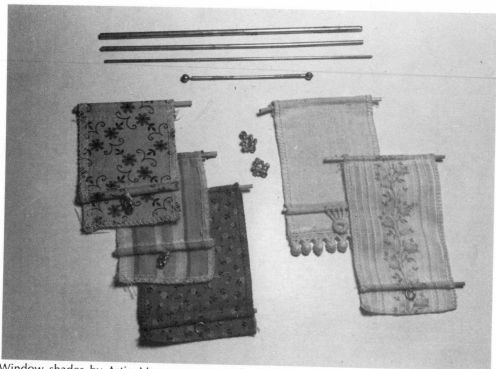

Window shades by Artie Marcus; pewter tiebacks from Colonial Craftsman; expandable curtain rod and plain brass rods from Mini Mundus lumberyard.

FRENCH DOORS

Materials

X-acto razor saw and miter box
White craft glue (Elmer's or Sobo)
2 strips basswood, $\frac{1}{8}'' \times \frac{5}{32}''$
2 strips $\frac{1}{8}''$ window sash (basswood)
1 strip basswood, $\frac{1}{16}'' \times \frac{1}{16}''$
1 sheet of .020 clear acetate, $8\frac{1}{2}'' \times 11''$
2 doorknobs
4 hinges

1. Cut out the side pieces of $\frac{1}{8}'' \times \frac{5}{32}''$ and $\frac{1}{8}''$ window sash and glue them together. Make sure that you leave the grooved side of the window sash showing. Allow to dry.
2. Cut out the end pieces of $\frac{1}{8}'' \times \frac{5}{32}''$ and $\frac{1}{8}''$ window sash and glue them together and allow to dry.
3. Cut five pieces of stripwood for mullions, $\frac{1}{16}'' \times \frac{1}{16}'' \times \frac{3}{4}''$.
4. Paint or stain all pieces at this time and allow to dry.

5. Glue the two short pieces to one of the side pieces, making sure that the grooves on the sash face the inside of the door-frame and that they align with the grooves in the side piece. Allow to dry.
6. Cut a piece of acetate $5\frac{23}{32}$" $\times$ $2\frac{7}{32}$" and insert into frame.
7. Glue the remaining side piece to the door.
8. Glue the mullions in place.
9. Mount the hardware to the door and hang in place.

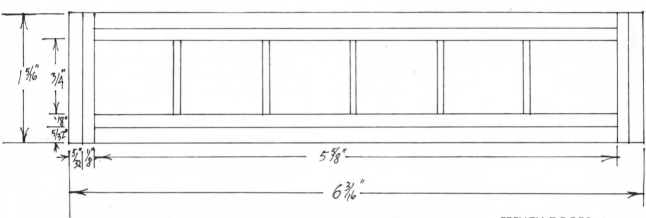

Mullions are $\frac{1}{16}$" $\times$ $\frac{1}{16}$" $\times$ $\frac{3}{4}$" Basswood / Space $\frac{7}{8}$"

$1\frac{5}{16}$" $\frac{3}{4}$" $\frac{1}{8}$" $\frac{5}{32}$" $\frac{5}{32}$" $\frac{1}{8}$" $5\frac{5}{8}$" $6\frac{3}{16}$"

FRENCH DOORS

French doors about to be installed in the Natasha Saypol dollhouse, under construction. Bamboo shades from Mini Mundus shop. Lace curtains add a formal touch to the French doors.

LOUVERED SHUTTERS

Materials

2 shutter frames $\frac{5}{32}$" basswood
1 basswood strip, $\frac{1}{32}$" × $\frac{5}{32}$"
1 sheet $\frac{1}{8}$" clapboard siding, $3\frac{1}{2}$" × 22"
X-acto razor saw and miter box
White craft glue (Elmer's or Sobo)

1. Cut the shutter frame $\frac{5}{32}$" to the dimensions in the plans and miter the ends of the pieces. Make certain that the original dimensions are measured from the outside of the mitered corners.
2. Cut two pieces of clapboard, $1\frac{5}{16}$" × $2\frac{3}{4}$".
3. Glue the sections of shutter frame together, leaving one side open as shown in the plans. Allow to dry.
4. Insert the pieces of clapboard into the frame and glue the remaining section of shutter frame to the shutter. Allow to dry.
5. Cut one piece of strip wood, $\frac{1}{32}$" × $\frac{5}{32}$" × $1\frac{3}{16}$", and glue to the shutter where the two pieces of clapboard meet. Allow to dry.
6. Stain or paint the colors of your choice.
7. The finished shutter will measure $5\frac{11}{16}$" × $1\frac{1}{2}$".

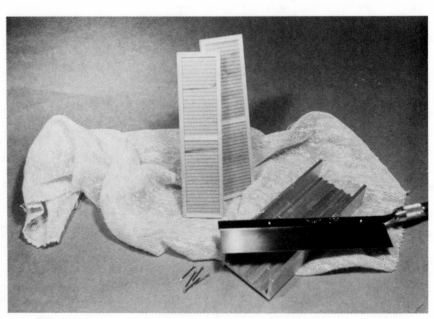

Louvered shutters complete most window settings. The mitered frame could also display shirred fabric for an armoire front. Miter box and saw from X-acto.

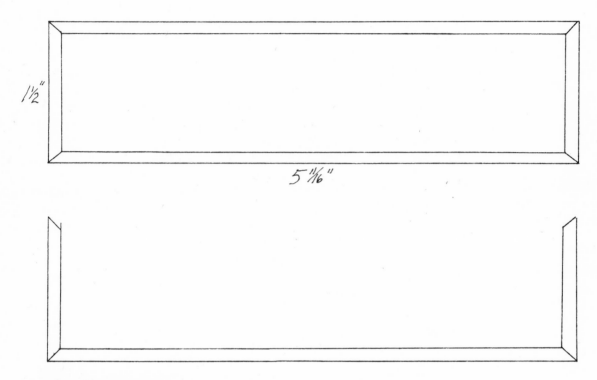

1½"

5 ¹¹⁄₁₆"

LOUVERED SHUTTERS

6

Inhabitants of Dollhouses

TYPES OF DOLLS

Just as most adults are five to six feet in height, "adult" dolls in a miniature setting should measure five to six inches ("child" dolls would measure proportionately).

The most beautiful dolls have head, hands, and feet made of painted porcelain, with muslin bodies. The hair is either molded porcelain or a wig that is glued on. Corinne Wilson[1] creates attractive mohair wigs, or you might use embroidery floss to design your own hair styles.

Another type of doll has a head fashioned from a round wooden bead, with hand-painted features. The bead is connected to a dowel or thick wire, to which the body is attached.

Another variation, again using a wooden bead, is to cover the bead with a layer of muslin. The facial features are then embroidered or painted onto the muslin.

You might prefer cutting the body and the head entirely from muslin and then stuffing the parts. Eyes, nose, and mouth can be painted. Eyebrows and sideburns are embroidered.

A favorite, of course, is the old-fashioned clothespin doll. The trick lies in delicately painting the features onto the head of a round wooden clothespin. The features should have the charming look of the old-fashioned dolls. Arms are created with pipe cleaners or wire.

It is best when dolls are flexible and can be put into sitting positions (the clothespin doll, of course, being the exception). This is why most dollmakers prefer muslin bodies. Some prefer inserting a pipe cleaner into the limbs in order to hold the position of the doll. Do you know a clever whittler? He/she could create wooden bodies with jointed elbows and legs. (If you sew seams at each joint on the muslin doll, the doll will be far more flexible. Vicky Newhouse does this. She sells her dolls in kits but it is difficult to duplicate her skill in sewing the bodies; they are beautifully proportioned. Muslin dolls' bodies must be well proportioned, otherwise the clothing will look lumpy.

If you have a kiln, you can buy standard dollhouse inhabitant molds (head, hands, and feet) from the Seeley Ceramic Company.

It is also possible to create a head out of papier mâché or Sculpey Clay. This clay, manufactured by the Polyform Company, bakes in a regular oven for thirty minutes. The charming results are ideal for a youngster's dollhouse family. Be sure to connect a dowel or thick wire to the clay head before baking, around which you will later attach the muslin body. You and your child can enjoy painting the head with simple features.

There is currently a new wave among crafters to create modeled-from-life reproductions. Many miniature enthusiasts enjoy having dolls in their own image inhabiting their dollhouses. Sandy Nardone and Lynn Sharp[4] have created a successful combination. Lynn fires the mold and hand paints the features. Sandy designs and sews the costumes. She encourages custom orders. She enjoys duplicating real-life families in miniature. Although the faces are limited, hair color and style, as well as costumes, come close to the model.

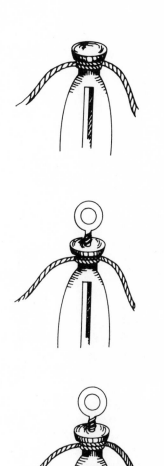

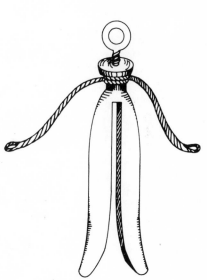

DOLL COSTUMES

Here are some tips from Bonnie McLean, who makes and dresses dolls at Mini Mundus.

When dressing miniature dolls, a better representation of clothing styles can be achieved by sewing costumes directly onto dolls rather than attempting removable clothing. The bulk of wider seams and clothing fasteners that are necessary for removable clothing is distracting. If you wish to be accurate to period and have had some experience adapting clothing patterns, there are some excellent costume books that give scale patterns and inspire examples.

CLOTHESPIN DOLLS
The head is made of modeling clay or papier maché built up on a screw eye. Arms are made of medium weight wire twisted around body of clothespin. With this type of clothespin, the only other material needed is a piece of medium weight wire for the arms, as the head is large enough to serve without any building up.

Wooden-head dolls.

English dolls by Lucy Stubbs. The heads are wooden beads covered with muslin. Features are embroidered and hand-painted.

Clothespin doll.

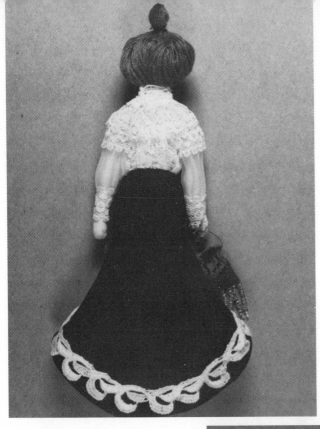

All muslin dolls by Carol Sligh.

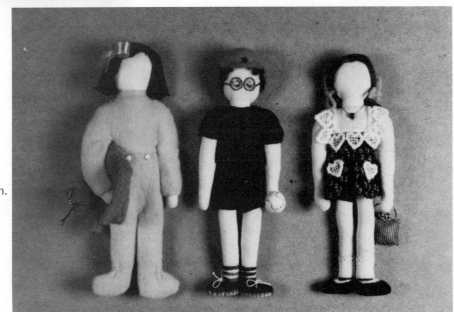

All muslin dolls by Carol Sligh.

All muslin dolls by Carol Sligh.

Betsy Ross muslin doll dressed by Marguerite Hatfield.

These books are often available through local libraries and bookstores: *Evolution of Fashion:* Pattern & Cut from 1066–1930, Hamilton Hill & Bucknell, Drama Books. *History of Costume,* Carl Kohler and Emma Von Sichart, Dover Press.

Delicate fabrics are most suitable and require little material. Remnants, scraps, and old clothing are the usual sources. If you intend to purchase fabric, consider the finer fabrics and trimmings. So little is required per doll that splurging does not set your budget back too far. A quarter yard of cloth will be ample for even the most elaborate costumes. On the other hand, make sure you have enough cloth to recut parts if necessary. Dressing miniature dolls requires a lot of experimenting.

If you use a relatively thick fabric such as wool flannel, hemming isn't necessary and would be obtrusively bulky. Dense fabrics that won't ravel, or are cut on the bias, can be cut at hem length. Or you can overcast one edge with matching thread.

Decorations such as bows, buttons, bits of lace, etc., can be glued. Once the fabric is sewn onto the doll, sewing these decorations is very difficult and doesn't always look as good when glued.

Sobo, used sparingly, works well on cloth. If the fabric you are using absorbs the glue easily, put a dot of glue on contact points of both parts, and allow to become tacky before pressing parts together.

One of the most intriguing aspects of miniature doll clothes is trims. Experiment with ideas that would be unlikely on a human scale. Trust your imagination. Trims are as important as the actual cut of the clothing and are useful in covering what you didn't mean to do.

Because doll clothing doesn't need the flexibility of human clothing, most pieces require very little shaping. If you aren't familiar with dressmaking, cut sections of garments in rectangles, or other general shapes, larger than the area you wish to cover. Pin to doll and little by little trim away excess, always smoothing the fabric over the form as you make each cut.

If you need two parts that are identical, such as right and left front, remove fitted pieces from doll and lay face-to-face on the material and cut matching part. Both parts can then be sewn onto the doll and you can proceed to the next part. Make sure you leave enough seam allowance to fold over the edges of previously sewn parts.

Only what will show is necessary to a costume that will be sewn onto a doll. For instance, if your "man" is wearing a suit, only the collar and cuffs and front of the shirt will show. So these are the only parts of the shirt that you need to make. In making the clothes, start with the parts that will be the layer closest to the body, and sew each successive layer over it.

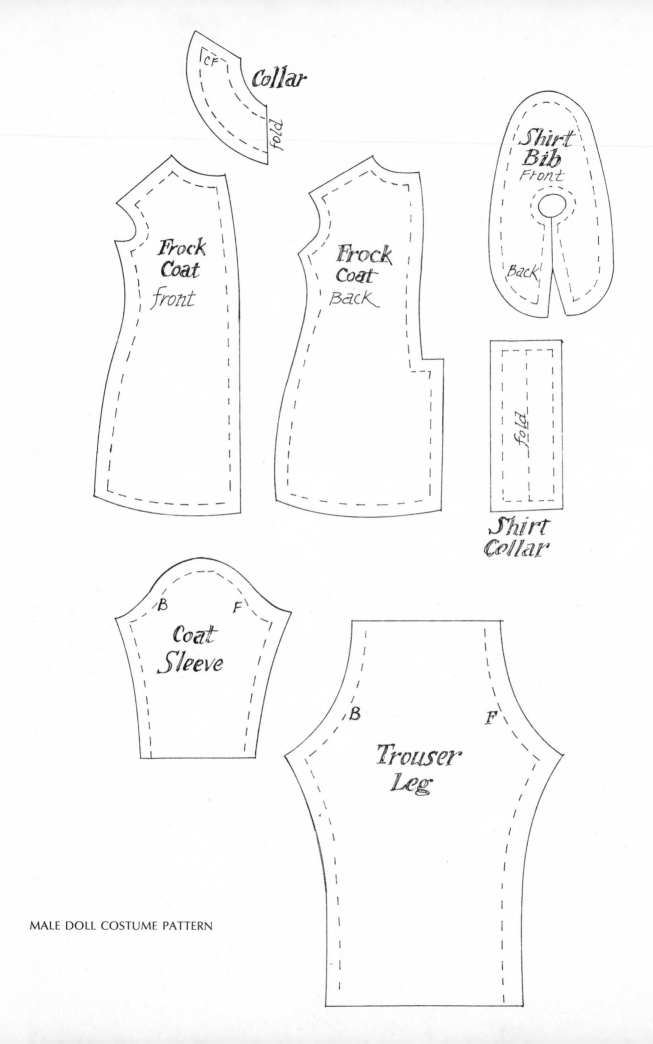

Collar

CF

fold

Frock
Coat
front

Frock
Coat
Back

Shirt
Bib
Front

Back

fold

Shirt
Collar

B   F

Coat
Sleeve

B   F

Trouser
Leg

MALE DOLL COSTUME PATTERN

Porcelain dolls by Lynn Sharp and Sandy Nardone; champagne bucket and tray by Brooke Tucker; brass candlestick from Clare-Bell Brassworks; hand-dipped candles and balloons from Mini Mundus shop.

Porcelain dolls by Lynn Sharp and Sandy Nardone; cradle and book from Mini Mundus shop.

Tom Antorino and his collection.

Antique dolls, old fabric, and accessories.

Porcelain dolls by Sandy Nardone and Lynn Sharp; stove and accessories from Mini Mundus shop.

Parts that stand away from the body, such as a full skirt, will have to be cut from measurements. Use a cloth tape measure, rather than a ruler. Stick to simple shapes and leave ample allowances. Try the cut pieces on the doll before stitching, hemming, or trimming.

Tom Antorino, of New York City, says he's a frustrated decorator, which explains his interest in dollhouse dolls and dollhouses. He has a lovely collection of dolls and seeks out antique ribbon, handkerchiefs, and lace in hard-to-find country junk shops. He feels that people who don't like old fabric on dolls make the biggest mistake when they replace the clothing. They diminish the value. He even looks for old ribbons from dresses of the twenties and thirties. Another good source is old trunk ribbons that were used to tie down clothes while traveling.

He likes to create displays with little antiques, such as the turn-of-the-century Christmas tree, once part of his grandparents' crèche scene. He decorated it beautifully with antique ribbon, mini candles, and strung beads.

143

Tom even prefers old thread, if it is strong enough to use, and ages his fabrics with tea to give a yellowed effect.

Like most enthusiastic miniaturists he has discovered little tricks. Using red felt, he cut out a man's vest and cut out two slits in the back to give a "tails" effect. Glued-on sparkles and sequins give the resemblance of jet beads. He always uses a tiny needle, so important in working with antique bits and pieces.

For authentic costumes he consults the Coleman Book (see Bibliography).

JIMMY'S CLOTHES—SHIRT AND TROUSERS

Cutting the Material

1. Take a 6″ square of lightweight fabric and fold it so you have a rectangle, 3″ × 6″.
2. Trace the shirt pattern onto the fabric, with the sleeve line along the fold. On this same piece of material trace the pattern for the shirt collar.

PATTERN FOR JIMMY CARTER DOLL

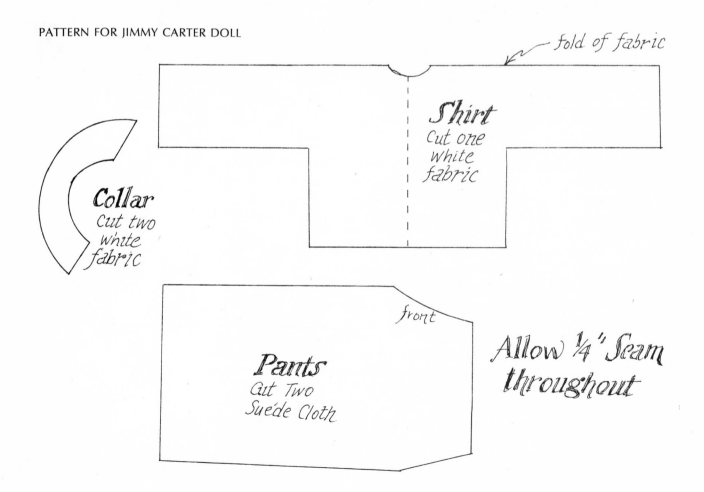

Jimmy Carter porcelain doll by Carol-Lynn Waugh. One of these dolls now resides in the White House, in Amy Carter's dollhouse.

3. Cut out the collar and shirt. When cutting out the shirt do not cut the fold. Cut two pieces of the pants pattern out of single-weight suede cloth. It is important to use single-weight cloth; double-weight cloth is too heavy.

Pants Construction

1. Seam the front; seam the back to the *X* marked on the pattern.
2. Sew the crotch together at the legs and turn right side out.

Shirt Construction

1. Glue the two collar pieces together with Sobo glue and allow to dry.
2. Fold the cuffs over ¼" to the wrong side of the shirt body. Machine sew at the inner edge, with the smallest stitch your machine is capable of doing.
3. Next sew each underarm seam, from wrist to waist. Clip at the underarms and turn right side out.
4. Place the shirt on the doll. Sew the shirt to the doll up the back with small stitches.
5. Sew the collar to the shirt. Sew four tiny beads to the cuffs, one on each side of the wrist, for buttons.

Finishing Touches

1. Cut a piece of leather ¼" × the waist measurement plus ½". Glue this piece to the waist and sew the ends together.
2. Cut four pieces of pants fabric $\frac{1}{16}$" × ¼" and glue them onto the pants for belt loops, two in the front and two in the back. One of the back loops should cover the seam in the belt.
3. The tie is ¼" velvet ribbon knotted at the top, sewn to the collar, and cut in a V at the belt.

COSTUMED MICE

The simplest sort of mouse to make is a gentleman mouse. The only materials needed to make one are black felt, a flower for his buttonhole (optional), and, of course, needle and thread. See pattern for instructions.

Another simple mouse to make is the "basic lady" (pattern B), shown in the photograph with matching green felt hat and skirt and a yellow, green, and white petticoat. She wears a silver bead for an earring (glued to her ear).

The angel mouse (shown) is more difficult to make than the others, but she makes a popular Christmas gift, as does the "basic lady," when done in traditional green and red with, perhaps, red or green feathers in her hat. The materials needed to make the angel mouse are yellow and white felt, gold sequin stars, and something for her to hold in her hand (if small gold instruments are not available, use your imagination!).

The other two mice shown are examples of the variations possible using pattern B. Both also make use of the basic dress of pattern C.

Mice in setting by Cynthia Stanton. Photograph by Peter Schaaf.

Costumed mouse by Cynthia Stanton.

Costumed mouse by Cynthia Stanton.

Costumed mouse by Cynthia Stanton.

Costumed mouse by Cynthia Stanton.

Costumed mouse by Cynthia Stanton.

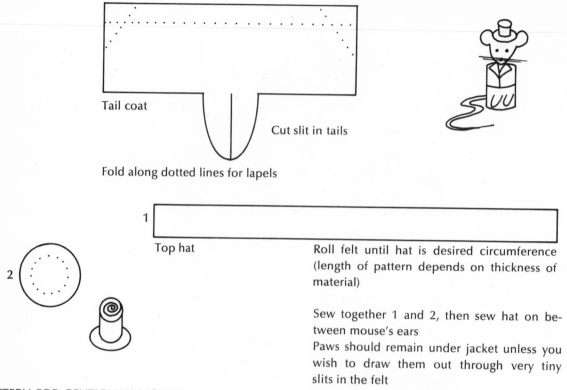

Tail coat

Cut slit in tails

Fold along dotted lines for lapels

1

Top hat

2

Roll felt until hat is desired circumference (length of pattern depends on thickness of material)

Sew together 1 and 2, then sew hat on between mouse's ears
Paws should remain under jacket unless you wish to draw them out through very tiny slits in the felt

PATTERN FOR GENTLEMAN MOUSE

(cut your own in accordance with size of mouse)

Mouse couturiere, Cynthia Stanton, a high school student, shares some patterns she has developed in her short but successful career.

The mice are commercially available in most toy shops.

PATTERN FOR LADY MOUSE

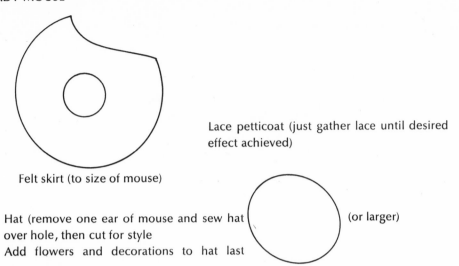

Felt skirt (to size of mouse)

Lace petticoat (just gather lace until desired effect achieved)

(or larger)

Hat (remove one ear of mouse and sew hat over hole, then cut for style
Add flowers and decorations to hat last

Pattern C—Christmas angel

Halo—yellow felt

white felt   Glue together

Front

Back   Sew star to back of yellow hat

Basic dress (adjust to size of mouse)

white felt

Holes for front paws

two skirts: cut two concentric circles out of white felt, one about ½ to ¾ inches smaller in diameter. Both should have holes in center for mouse as in drawing
Decorate top skirt (a) with stars

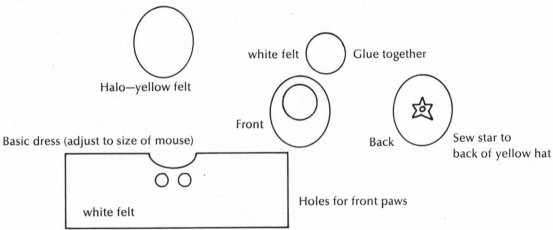

a   b   a b

Wings (yellow felt)
Sew to basic dress

7
Accessories

Barabara Hackney creating ribbon pillows.

EDWARDIAN TOWELS

(No Sewing Necessary!)

Barbara Hackney has been creating accessories for Mini Mundus for several years. Here are some tips from her expertise.

If you have an old damask napkin, old-fashioned linen hock guest towel, or a decoratively edged hankie that you are willing to cut up, you can make beautiful "correct" towels for your Victorian or Edwardian dollhouse. (There was no terry cloth in those days.) Find a section on the fabric that has a pleasing design in miniature. Cut out a piece approximately 1½" wide × 2½" long, utilizing the edge of the piece as the border of the little towel, or find a section of design on the interior of the fabric (see sketch).

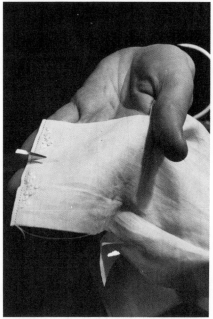

Close-up of handkerchief used to cut out miniature towels.

EDWARDIAN TOWELS

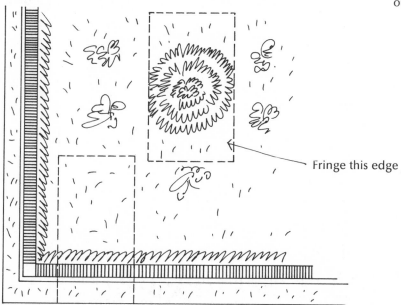

Fringe this edge

Two ways to cut towels from a napkin or handkerchief, making use of existing patterns and edging

Fold and press

Fold and press

Fold and press

Pull threads to make fringe

Fold and press

Fold under and press as shown in sketches. Fringe one end if you are using an interior piece. There is no need to hem the other three sides, since they are folded under and will not show. These towels look marvelous on your miniature towel rack.

CURTAINS

(Dainty and Properly Limp)

It is usually difficult to find new fabric soft and limp enough to hang well in a dollhouse when used as curtains, tablecloths, or bedcovers. One way to solve the problem is to use very old handkerchiefs that have been washed many, many times. The decorative borders on many hankies look wonderful when used as curtains. Just cut and gather to fit your windows.

RUGS FROM UPHOLSTERY FABRIC

(No Sewing Necessary!)

Rugs can be quickly and cheaply made by finding a scrap of upholstery fabric with a pattern that suggests a rug design in the size you want. Cut out the rug shape plus about ¼″ extra all around. Apply a piece of fusible Pellon to the underside of the fabric with a hot iron. When fused fabric and Pellon cool, trim with scissors to desired size. The Pellon discourages fraying.

If the rug shape is rectangular or square, you can have fringe on two or four sides. For this, the Pellon should be cut the exact size of the rug and applied with care, placing it exactly. Then you pull the threads on the ¼″ of excess fabric. I found an upholstery fabric with a pattern of rectangles that looked exactly like little oriental rugs.

PILLOWS

Charming boxed pillows can be made from velvet or satin ribbon, or from those beautiful embroidered tapes. Cut 1″-wide ribbon into two 1½″ lengths. Fold and press each row end under ¼″. Cut ¼″-wide ribbon in same or contrasting color long enough to go all around plus ½″ (approximately 4½″ long). Neatly sew, with tiny stitches, the sides and the front and back together, leaving enough space to insert stuffing (be sure to get into the corners). Finish closing up (see sketch).

RIBBON PILLOW
NEEDLEPOINT AND LACE PILLOW

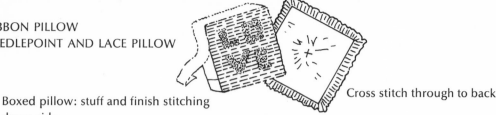

Boxed pillow: stuff and finish stitching
down side

Cross stitch through to back

First fold
blind-stitch
down

Second fold
blind-stitch down

Third fold
blind-stitch
down

Fourth fold
blind-stitch down

Instructions for ½" embroidered tape pillow.
Add sides, back, and stuffing

The front side of the pillow can be cut from the decorative
tape. Or work a square of petit point. With petit point, fold ¼"
excess canvas under and glue or stitch down. Attach the side ribbon to edge petit point stitches.

Narrow ribbons or decorative tapes can give a different look
to the pillow front by folding into four corners and stitching down
as shown in sketches and photo. A tiny button can be sewn on at
the center, stitching all the way through pillow.

The easiest pillows to make require simply stitching the front
and back together, with no side strip, which can be difficult to do
neatly.

A lace-edged pillow for the dollhouse bedroom is made by
shirring some very delicate ribbon lace and tucking this between
the front and back of the pillow as you sew them together.

CROCHET AND LACE TABLECLOTH

A tablecloth can be made from a rectangular piece of sturdy lace fabric (used for making an article of clothing). Work with crochet floss or sewing thread.

You can treat this lace fabric as if it is a foundation chain. Some call it edging. Once you have completed the first round, you can create any edging you want.

Crochet and lace tablecloth by Rebecca Mercer-White.

TABLECLOTH AND NAPKINS

Measure your tabletop and cut your cloth (batiste is best) ½″ wider around the edges. Glue fine lace around the edges using Sobo glue. Decorate with green and red cutouts for Christmas.

For napkins, cut six 1¼″ squares of the same fine material. Cut small narrow strips from colored paper to form napkin ring material. Roll the small strip around the rolled napkins and glue the ends together.

CHRISTMAS STOCKING

Usually a Christmas stocking hangs from a mantel. Measure your miniature fireplace to choose the correct length stocking.

Draw the pattern twice on a piece of felt. Cut out with pinking shears. Sew or glue pieces together.

This particular stocking was created from pink felt with a pink satin ribbon used as trim. A plastic charm toy sticks out from the top.

PLACE MATS AND NAPKINS

Using a straight sc stitch, ch until desired width is reached, then ch 1 and turn. Sc in second ch from hook and continue to sc until end of row. Ch 1 and turn. Follow in this manner until rectangle is achieved.

FABRIC BREAD BASKET

Gauge according to the size of your french loaves, and cut three rectangular pieces of cardboard for the bottom and long sides. Cut two square pieces for both ends.

Glue pieces of cardboard together. Cover with tiny-patterned fabric. Allow ⅛″ for seam. A stiff trim is used for the handle.

CROCHETED WASTEBASKET OR PLANTER

Ch 10; join ch with sl st into a ring. Ch 1; hdc into each ch in rnd. Continue in a spiral. Add "tassel"—double-knotted crochet threads.

Christmas dinner scene. Cloth and napkins by Kathe LaTour; Christmas tree centerpiece under dome by Brooke Tucker; silver tableware by Clare-Bell Brassworks; Christmas stocking by Hope Elliott.

Place mats by Barbara Hackney; fabric bread basket by Kathe La-Tour; other accessories from Mini Mundus shop.

Crocheted macramé holder by Barbara Hackney. Toothbrush and glass by Alice Robbins.

TERRY CLOTH BATH MAT

In proportion with the scale of your bathroom, measure a rectangle onto desired color of lightweight terry cloth, allowing for hem. Turning edge under, stitch entire rectangle ⅛″ in from turned edge. Trim with strip of narrow velvet ribbon, placed diagonally across one corner.

TERRY CLOTH TOWEL

Cut two rectangular pieces of lightweight terry cloth. Hem the two short edges with a basting stitch, then trim with velvet ribbon and lace.

Terry cloth towels and bath mat by Shep's Designery.

TERRY CLOTH BATH SLIPPERS

In proportion with your bath mat, or using your doll's feet as a pattern, cut two slippers from terrycloth. Stitch entire edge. A small piece of narrow velvet ribbon is added as a strap.

CORSET

Measure the girth of your doll. The corset should reach from below bosom to abdomen. Trim with lace (can be glued on).

Use an eyelet punch to insert metal eyelets. Tie with a narrow shoestring or similar material.

orset by Lady Jayne Miller. Pearls by Mikimoto.

Felt hat by Joen Ellen Kanze. Petit point cushion and chair by Amanda Bartlett.

HATS

Joen Ellen Kanze is able to achieve a tremendous variety of hats using felt, fake flowers, feathers, and glue.

Cut one circle for the brim, approximately 1½" in diameter. From the center of this circle, cut a hole ⅝" in diameter. Split the brim from the hole to the outside. Overlap the ends and glue, helping to give it shape. Cut a ½"-wide "fence" from the felt and glue to the brim. The round piece cut from the center is the crown and is now placed on top of the "fence" and glued. All trims are later glued to the "fence" and brim.

MINIATURE KNITTING

You will need two enamel-tipped pins, matching-color, mercerized, cotton-covered polyester thread, and a knowledge of knitting!

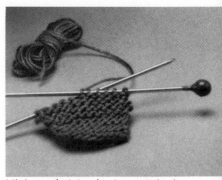

Miniature knitting by Susan Teltscher

Make a loop around one pin and tie the thread quite tightly to create the first stitch. It's not necessary to knot it on. Don't leave too long an end, as it will get in the way. Cast on sixteen or seventeen stitches. Circling the thread around the index finger can make the procedure easier.

At the end of the first row, slip the last stitch or two, leaving at least fifteen stitches with which to work. Use this short piece of thread, from the slipped stitches, to twist into a loose knot that can be pushed all the way down until it meets the last stitch taken. It can be doubled, if desired, before being pulled tight, but must not stick out more than absolutely necessary.

Knit eight to ten rows, until the work measures between ⅛″ and ¼″. Then, knit halfway across one row and leave the needles crisscrossed in the middle of a stitch. Leave an inch of straight thread, from the last completed stitch.

Then, wrap the thread, from the spool with which you've been working, around the index finger eighteen times or so. Slide these small circles of thread off the finger, keeping them as close together as possible, and detach the piece from the spool. Cut an additional 2″ length of thread. Use this to tie together the middle section of the circles of thread, making them in two bowlike loops, resembling a mini skein of wool. Eighteen circles O of thread before tying thusly 8 2″.

Then place in 2″ × 2″ plastic (jeweler's) bag and tape shut.

VELVET PHOTOGRAPH ALBUM

This project requires a piece of velvet 2⅓″ long and 1½″ wide, some cardboard of the same dimensions, and gold paint.

Cut cardboard into two halves and glue the halves to underside of velvet. Paint cardboard with gold paint—this is the inside cover of album. Leave room on velvet for the spine, for opening and closing.

Fold brown paper for "leaves." Cut oval shape to display miniature photos.

Velvet photograph album by Caroline Bugg.
Felt plumed hat by Joen Ellen Kanze.

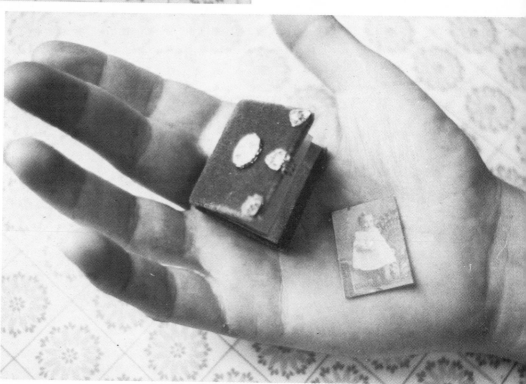

Close-up of album.

MINIATURE SEWING BOX

Sewing box from Mini Mundus. Mini sampler kits by June Dole.

CROSS-STITCH SAMPLERS

Cross-stitch sampler from June Dole. There are forty-eight stitches to the inch!

Bibliography

BOOKS

The ABC's of Needlepoint. Hope Hanley. New York: Scribner, 1973.

Cabinetmaker's Guide. Four volumes are available from Calico Print Shop, 4712-C E. Central, Wichita, Kansas 67208. Includes a few upholstered pieces. Inquire also about their journal *The Scale Cabinetmaker,* usually issued seasonally.

Early North American Dollmaking. Iris Sanderson Jones. New York: Charles Scribner's, 1977. A narrative history and craft instructions, folk type.

Fun with Needlepoint. Hope Hanley. New York: Scribner, 1972.

Miniature Needlepoint Rugs for Dollhouses. Susan McBand. New York: Dover Publications, 1976.

Needlework in Miniature. Virginia Merrill and Jean Jessop. New York: Crown Publications, 1978.

Needlework Stitches. Barbara Snook. New York: Crown Publications, 1963.

On Making, Mending, and Dressing Dolls. Clara Hallard Fawcett. Hobby House Press, 4701 Queensbury Road, Riverdale, Maryland 20840. Free catalogue, large selection of books on dolls. 1977 reprint.

Petit Needlecraft. Linda Lea Kaufmann. Stone Mountain, Georgia: Craft Publications, 1976. $2.50.

Stitchery, Needlepoint, Appliqué & Patchwork: A Complete Guide.
Shirley Marien. New York: Viking Press, 1974.
This Side of Yesteryear. Catherine MacLaren. Many photographs,
and special section on history of furniture. A useful decorating
guide, written by one of the nicest ladies in the miniature world.
Order from the author, 1035 Newkirk Drive, La Jolla, California
92037. $10.
The Collector's Book of Doll's Clothes: Costumes in Miniature,
1700–1929. New York: Crown Publications, 1975.

MAGAZINES

Dollhouse and Miniature News, 3 Orchard Lane, Kirkwood,
Missouri 63122.
International Dollhouse News, 56 Lincoln Wood, Haywards Heath,
Sussex RH16 1LM, England.
The Miniature Collector, 170 Fifth Avenue, New York, New York
10010.
Miniature Gazette, published four times a year by N.A.M.E. (National Association of Min Enthusiasts), P.O. Box 2621, Anaheim,
California 92804.
Nutshell News, 1035 Newkirk Drive, La Jolla, California 92037.
Small Talk, P.O. Box 334, Laguna Beach, California 92651. $10. a
year for 12 issues; sample copy $1.

Appendix: Custom Work, Catalogues and Listings

CUSTOM WORK

These fine crafters create fine reproductions of antique furniture. Their catalogues and lists include upholstered pieces as well. (SASE is a self-addressed, stamped envelope.)

Hermania Anslinger
320 South Ralph Street
Spokane, Washington 99202
Send SASE for list,
$1.50 for photos.

Chestnut Hill Studio
Box 38
Churchville, New York 14428
Send $3 for catalogue.

Thomas Deveraux
Hollywood Tower, Apt. 27
5701 N. Sheridan Road
Chicago, Illinois 60660
Specializes in Victoriana.

Donald Dube
960 East Broadway
Woodmere, New York 11598
Send SASE and $.50 for list.

Dolphin Originals
Robert Bernhard
7302 Hasbrook Avenue
Philadelphia, Pennsylvania
19111
Send $1 for list, $.50 for
photos.

Virginia Merrill
Blue Swan Studio
Lee's Hill Road
New Vernon, New Jersey 07976
Send SASE for list.

Mrs. Mell Prescott
Box 177
Warrenville, Connecticut 06278

Terry Rogal
166 East 96th Street
New York, New York 10021

Mrs. Dorothy Wade
132 Belle Crest Avenue
East Northport, New York
11731
Send SASE for reply.

Willoughby's
P.O. Box 918
Los Altos, California 94022
Send $2 for catalogue.
Specializes in 18th century.

CATALOGUES AND LISTINGS

Alnap Co., Inc.
65 Reade Street, New York, New York 10007
Sells in quantity. Craft sticks, wood beads, doll head beads and eyes, metal findings, needles, etc. Request catalogue and mention you want to buy in quantity—otherwise your request may be ignored.

Arlene Bellinger
5521 East Morris
Wichita, Kansas 67218
Hats and flowers, very authentic and painstakingly made.
Send long SASE.

Boutique Margot
26 West 54th Street
New York, New York 10019
29 mesh per inch, 40" wide $38 per yard
38 mesh per inch, 40" wide $38 per yard
48 mesh per inch, 40" wide $50 per yard
58 mesh per inch, 40" wide $50 per yard
Sold as follows: 9" × 20"   9" × 40"   18" × 40"   27" × 40"
                    36" × 40"
Source for Appleton wool. Add $1 for postage and handling.

Caroline Bugg
957 North Dellrose
Wichita, Kansas 67208
Created the velvet photograph album. Send SASE for listing, which includes baskets and meats.

Claudia's Doll House
P.O. Box 135
Elmgrove, Louisiana 71051
Dresden quality porcelain dolls, including reproduction of dollhouse Bru doll. Send SASE and $.50.

Create Your Own
Box 393
Peapack, New Jersey 07977
Catherine Knowles is the designer of this wonderful line of miniature needlepoint. Send SASE for a listing of kits and prices.

Margaret Dilley
112 South Shelly Drive
Ashbourne Hills
Claymont, Delaware 19703
Makes unusual rugs by using a miniature latch-hook (intended for correcting snags in knit materials) and knotting sport-weight yarn onto needlepoint canvas then clipping evenly. Send SASE for listing.

June Dole
1280 North Stone
West Suffield, Connecticut 06093
Send SASE for brochure on mini sampler kits, completed samplers, and mini pillows. Charming!

Tori Layne Foster
P.O. Box 135
Elmgrove, Louisiana 71051
Includes linens, draperies, and curtains in her listing. Send SASE and $.50.

Vicki Fox
2128 Delancey Place
Philadelphia, Pennsylvania 19103
Send SASE and $.25 for list of hand-painted canvases.

Rene and Judy Gaillardetz
P.O. Box 575
Marlboro, Massachusetts 01732
Miniature needlework, fine crochet, petit point rugs. Send SASE.

Evelyn Gerratana
24 Chestnut Hill Road
Trumbull, Connecticut 06611
Creates unusual hand-painted velvet rugs. Husband Frank makes a wonderful steamer trunk with drawers and hangers, the kind that opera singers use when traveling transatlantic!

Dotty Gulker
c/o Mini Mundus Shop
1030 Lexington Avenue
New York, New York 10021
Send SASE for listing.

Barbara Hackney
75 Henry Street
Brooklyn, New York 11201
Edwardian towels, pillows of linen and cotton, etc.
Send SASE and $.25.

Hand and Heart Crafts
P.O. Box 1072
Mount Vernon, Illinois 62864
Candle screen, fireside screen, gout stool; made of solid walnut,
either the rose or foulard pattern on the petit point pieces. Send
long SASE.

Herrschner
Hoover Road
Steven Point, Wisconsin 54481
Offers free catalogue of needlework supplies. Send long SASE.

Hook and Needle
17 Wall Street
Huntington, New York 11743
Specializes in dolls and doll clothing. Send SASE.

Isn't It (A Small World)
2121 East Third
Tulsa, Oklahoma 74009
Clever selection of accessories, such as long red underwear, etc.
Send SASE and $.50.

It's A Small World
542 Lincoln Avenue
Winnetka, Illinois 60093
Finished upholstered pieces included in this fine selection. Send
$2 for catalogue.

Jean Jessop
64 Blackburn Road
Summit, New Jersey 07901
Custom-made tapestries, petit point rugs. Send SASE with
request.

Fran Kirkland's Needlework
16930 Kercheral Avenue
Grosse Pointe, Michigan 48230
Carries needlepoint kits and materials.

Lynn Kusnet
2100 Linwood Avenue
Fort Lee, New Jersey 07024
Upholsters sofas; has access to tiny prints through her decorating business. Send SASE.

Kathe LaTour
166 West 76th Street
New York, New York 10023
Creates curtains, drapes, tablecloths, napkins, spreads, etc. Send SASE with request.

Sue Lerner
500 Franklin Turnpike
Ridgewood, New Jersey 07450
Curtains, bedspreads, and pillows. Send SASE and $.25.

Marion A. Lomaglio
Box 432
Westwood, New Jersey 07675
American samplers, dolls. Send SASE.

Patti Machen
15111 Paseo Flores
Saratoga, California 95070
Specializes in miniature doll wigs. Send SASE and $1.

Marribee
2904 West Kabcaster
Fort Worth, Texas 76107
Offers free catalogue of needlework supplies. Send SASE.

Bonnie McLean
c/o Stone Hill Studio
Box 94
Stonington, Connecticut 06378
Custom needlework. Send SASE with your request.

Lady Jayne Miller
1766 West San Carlos
San Jose, California 95126
408-287-7127
Doll collector extraordinaire. Repairs bisque and composition dolls, creates authentic costumes and accessories, and conducts classes in costume making. Send SASE and $1.

Mini Mundus Lumberyard
970 Lexington Avenue
New York, New York 10021
212-288-5855
Building materials, needlepoint and furniture kits, windows, doors, hardware, etc. Send $3 for catalogue. Includes finished miniatures, too.

Mini Mundus Shop
1030 Lexington Avenue
New York, New York 10021
212-288-5855
Dolls, rugs, curtains, furnishings, and accessories.

Miniature Coverlets
Lillian A. Gaines
212 South Sixth Street
Independence, Kansas 67301
Exact reproduction of a "snowballs" pattern. Send SASE for a complete listing.

Needleworks In Miniature
Ms. Barbara Glass
P.O. Box 28041
Atlanta, Georgia 30328
A beautiful array of available patterns, hand-painted canvases. Send $2 for catalogue.

Vicky Newhouse
20402 Grayston Lane
Huntington Beach, California 92646

Priscilla's Doll House
44 West Home Street
Westerville, Ohio 43081
Quilts, caning, etc. Send SASE for list.

Rose Ries
10531 Wellworth Avenue
Los Angeles, California 90024
213-474-3810
Custom sewing of finest fabrics and pure silk. Sheet sets, cotton chintz set of double spread with matching pillow and quilt, spreads of blue-and-white ticking with little embroidery. Send SASE or stamp. She prefers to answer letters personally.

Doll Dress Making by Sandy
289 Brook Avenue
North Plainfield, New Jersey 07060
Send SASE for list.

Seeley Ceramic Co.
9 River Street
Oneonta, New York 13820
Dollhouse molds as seen in Victorian porcelain dolls. Necessary to have access to kiln.

Selma's Art Needlework
1645 Second Avenue
New York, New York 10028
Handles Marlitt rayon floss (4 strands), 38 and 48 mesh cotton, Penelope canvas. Send SASE for list.

Lynn Sharp
289 Brook Avenue
North Plainfield, New Jersey 07060
Dollhouse kits, porcelain heads, hands, and feet. Send SASE for list.

Doreen Sinnett Designs
418 Santa Ana Avenue
Newport Beach, California 92660
Mini hooker for rug making, many patterns available. Send SASE for rug making listings.

Mary Skofield
P.O. Box 562
Haywood, California 94543
A "body builder" of sawdust-stuffed dollhouse dolls! Send SASE and $.50.

Sally Smith
86 Church Street
Hudson, Ohio 44236
Specializes in hooked rugs. Send SASE for price list.

Kay Sobers's Creations
2086 Fairwood Lane, NE
Atlanta, Georgia 30345
Hand-painted canvases: traditional, oriental and contemporary. Several of her creations are in the Cornelia Vanderbilt Whitney dollhouse. Send SASE and $1 for designs.

Corinne Taylor
1700B West Granville Street
Chicago, Illinois 60660
Lifelike dolls made to order; finely detailed, authentically costumed. Send SASE.

Mitzi Van Horn
8205 Buffalo Avenue
Norfolk, Virginia 23518
Fantastic petit point! Send SASE for list.

Vonnie's Babes
116 Taylor Street
Santa Cruz, California 95060
Porcelain family dolls. Send SASE and $.50.

Rebecca Mercer-White
1174 Second Avenue
New York, New York 10021
Crocheted curtains, spreads, tablecloths, etc. Send SASE and $.25.

Carol-Lynn Waugh
5 Morrill Street
Winthrop, Maine 04364
Jimmy Carter and Victorian porcelain dolls. Send SASE.

Willow Tree Arts & Crafts
747 Delaware Street
Sheridan Plaza
Tonawanda, New York 14223
Heirloom quality rugs and needlework. Send SASE.

Corinne Wilson
2608 Cheyenne
Wichita, Kansas 67216
Specializes in mohair wigs—dark brown, medium brown, blonde, and gray; variety of styles. Send SASE for listing.

Yo's Needlecraft
1825 Post
Japanese Cultural Center
San Francisco, California 94115
415-567-3334
Send long SASE for complete listing of Japanese symbol needle-work books. Very helpful proprietress!

Index